SHOULD
CHRISTIANS BE
ENVIRONMENTALISTS?

ALSO BY DAN STORY

Defending Your Faith, Kregel Publications
Christianity on the Offense, Kregel Publications
Engaging the Closed Minded, Kregel Publications
The Christian Combat Manual, AMG Publishers
Where Wild Things Live, Naturegraph Publishers
Plus fifteen apologetics booklets, Joy Publishing

SHOULD CHRISTIANS BE ENVIRONMENTALISTS?

DAN STORY

Kregel
Publications

Portions of chapter 3 were originally published in Dan Story, "Are Animists Model Environmentalists?" *Christian Research Journal* 33, no. 2 (May/June 2010), 44–51.

Portions of chapters 5 and 8 were originally published in Dan Story, "Should Christians Be Environmentalists?" *Christian Research Journal* 33, no. 4 (September/October 2010), 19–27.

Library of Congress Cataloging-in-Publication Data
Story, Dan
Should Christians be environmentalists? : helping Christians see why caring for the earth matters, helping environmentalists see why Christianity matters / Dan Story.
    p. cm.
Includes bibliographical references (p. 185).
1. Human ecology—Religious aspects—Christianity. 2. Ecotheology. 3. Nature—Religious aspects—Christianity. I. Title.
BT695.5.S76   2012   261.8'8—dc23   2011045216

ISBN 978-0-8254-4249-0

Printed in the United States of America

12 13 14 15 16 / 5 4 3 2 1

To my daughter, Jody.
Some of my fondest memories are family hikes
and backpacks through woods and deserts
during your wonderful childhood years.

CONTENTS

Contents

INTRODUCTION

Oh, how I wish I had wings like a dove;
then I would fly away and rest!
I would fly far away
to the quiet of the wilderness.
King David, Psalm 55:6–7 (NLT)

I rushed into young adulthood during the turbulent years of the 1960s. I remember it well. On November 22, 1963, my first year in college, I was cutting classes with two buddies to escape to the mountains when we heard on the car radio that President John F. Kennedy had been assassinated. A few years later, in 1968, his brother Robert F. Kennedy and civil rights leader Martin Luther King Jr. were also assassinated. The Vietnam War became enormously unpopular in the late 1960s, and student protests erupted on university campuses. Race riots rocked American society. The sixties spawned the "flower children" in Haight-Ashbury, San Francisco, the countercultural music at Woodstock in New York State (1969), and a burgeoning drug culture that threatened to hemorrhage the moral values of America's youth. Thousands of disillusioned young people became hippie dropouts.

Historians report that no society in the history of the human race has changed as dramatically or as quickly as American culture has during the last decades of the twentieth century. It all evolved out of the sociological upheavals of the 1960s. Within a mere forty years, American society shifted from a largely Christian world-and-life view to a secular worldview.

April 22, 1970—barely into a new decade—marked another event that arose out of the 1960s: the first "Earth Day." Twenty million Americans assembled across two thousand colleges and universities, thousands of primary and secondary schools, and hundreds of local communities to create a grassroots groundswell for an environmental movement unprecedented in its scope and enthusiasm. A new awareness of the interrelatedness of all life—plants, animals, and humans—and the deterioration of our air, water, land, and natural resources galvanized America's youth. And I discovered my calling.

Unlike my brother, who spent part of the 1960s in a commune on the Olympic Peninsula in Washington State, I didn't become a hippie. I didn't protest the Vietnam War. I didn't get into drugs. My wife didn't wear flowers in her hair (although she put flower decals on the body of our 1966 Datsun station wagon). But I did plunge into the environmental movement of the 1970s with all the passion and zeal of youth. My wife and I joined the Sierra Club and the National Wildlife Federation. We backpacked, photographed wildlife, and supported environmental causes. We volunteered at a wildlife rescue center. I published more than thirty wildlife and nature related articles in magazines and other periodicals. My music of choice was John Denver. I was energized and inspired by "Rocky Mountain High," "Take Me Home, Country Roads," "Sunshine on My Shoulders," and "Blow Up Your TV." I spent countless hours listening to Denver's music in my study and on the tape player in my car. We lived in Southern California but craved to live in wild country. I seriously considered quitting my job and moving my family to the outskirts of Zion National Park. My wife was all for it. In short, as a non-Christian, nature was my life.

This changed dramatically in 1981 after I became a Christian. My love for nature was quickly overshadowed by my love for the Creator. It was not that my love and enthusiasm for nature diminished—it was just no longer the center of my life. In fact, my thesis for a master's degree in Christian apologetics was a 330-page tome entitled *Environmental Stewardship: A Biblical Approach to Environmental Ethics.* After graduating in 1988, however, my focus in writing changed. Instead of nature themes, I took up the case for Jesus Christ and began to write books and teach classes on how to defend the Christian faith.

During the ensuing years, I periodically yearned to resume my writing about nature, wildlife, and the environment. I envisioned that a book on a subject like "Encountering God in the Wilderness" or "Is God an Environmentalist?" would be a great apologetic point of contact with secular nature lovers and environmentalists. But the time never seemed right to begin such a project. Nor could I imagine such a book having broad appeal in the Christian community, which historically has shown little interest in environmental matters and has often opposed environmental activism.[1]

In recent years, however, there has been a growing concern over environmental issues within Christendom, including among evangelicals. In part, this is because diverse political and scientific views on climate change (global warming) have spawned much confusion and misinformation, intensifying environmental debates and adding to the hostility that already existed between conservatives and left-leaning environmentalists.

This, however, is not a book detailing environmental issues; nor is it a doomsayer's appraisal of potential environmental catastrophes. Enough is already being written on those topics. Rather, the primary purpose of this book is threefold. First, to encourage godly environmental stewardship by systematically developing a Bible-based theology of nature, including an environmental doctrine and guidelines for environmental ethics. What does an environmental doctrine reveal? Among other things, it reveals that the Bible instructs the human race to be God's caretakers over creation. It provides moral principles that can guide mankind's activities in nature so that people use the earth's resources without selfishly exploiting the land and its wild inhabitants.

The second primary purpose of *Should Christians Be Environmentalists?* is to present an apologetic to anti-Christian environmentalists who claim that Christianity is the "root cause" of environmental exploitation and degradation, and that other religious traditions are better suited morally and theologically to push for environmental stewardship.

In answer to these and other challenges, we'll discover that every culture, regardless of religious beliefs, has exploited and despoiled its natural environment. We'll establish that God directed the entire human race to be His caretakers—His stewards—over nature. He didn't give mankind carte blanche to use nature with no concern for the land and other life forms. I'll demonstrate that Christianity, more than any other worldview—secular or religious—is equipped to implement and institutionalize worldwide environmental ethics. The book includes strategies for how the church can engage corporately in proactive environmental stewardship activities and how individual Christians can put into practice sensible measures that will contribute solutions to local environmental problems. We'll also explore the potential evangelistic opportunities embedded in Christian environmentalism.

Let me comment further on this last topic; it's the third purpose of this book.

Evangelistic and apologetic techniques that were effective thirty years ago, such as rational arguments and historical evidences for the Christian faith, are not as effective in the twenty-first century. In particular, people under the age of thirty have been conditioned by postmodern relativism to reject moral absolutes and to be skeptical of all religious truth claims. Accordingly, Christian evangelists and apologists are urgently seeking relevant "points of contact"—areas of common concern to both Christians and non-Christians—that can be starting points for conversations, often leading to opportunities for sharing the gospel message.

Stephen Rand of the Evangelical Alliance Relief Fund reports, "Every survey showed that the environment was top of the list of [young people's] concerns for the future, for the planet."[2] In light of this, I'm convinced that Christian environmentalism can be a tremendously effective point of contact with this generation, especially among college students and other young people.

I conclude the book with a special word to non-Christian readers. I share my journey from zealous non-Christian environmental advocate to even more zealous Christian environmentalist, and the impact this journey has had on my life. My story can become the reader's story.

My prayer is that, as you work your way through this book, you'll not only develop a better understanding of the biblical perspective of environmental stewardship, but that you'll also come to better love and enjoy God's magnificent creation in the process.

PART ONE

ENVIRONMENTALISM: A MOVEMENT IN NEED OF A RELIGION

CHAPTER ONE

WHAT EVER HAPPENED TO THE ENVIRONMENTAL MOVEMENT?

Environmentalist: A person who is concerned with or
advocates the protection of the environment.
The New Oxford American Dictionary

H anging on my study walls are paintings and photographs of national parks and other wild places: Yellowstone, Zion, and
Glacier National Parks; the Sierra Nevada mountains in eastern
California; Monument Valley in southern Utah; the Rocky Mountains.
All of them are places I have visited—and often explored—and long to
see again. In my whimsical moods, I imagine these pictures as windows to
the wilderness. I envision myself climbing through their frames and walking the wild lands beyond.

As pleasurable as these daydreams are, they're always clouded with a
grave concern. Will these great tracts of American wilderness continue
to exist, so that future nature wanderers can experience their solace and
solitude? Not if many developers have their way. Yosemite Valley, the outskirts of Zion National Park, the south rim of the Grand Canyon—all are
threatened by hotel and commercial development.

A similar desire to explore wild nature is awakened when I visit art
museums. My favorite painters are the Romantics (ca. 1750–1850), who
envisioned nature as boundless, untamed, and sublime. Their paintings typically create exaggerated, almost mythical portrayals of wild nature: colossal, jagged mountains with cloud-draped, snow-capped peaks.
Raging, boiling, angry rivers with stalwart explorers pondering safe

crossing. Dark, misty, forbidden, impenetrable forests where dwell fierce grizzlies, crowned elk, and glorious soaring eagles. Like the paintings and photographs on my study walls, these portrayals of wild nature invoke a powerful urge to plunge into the primeval wilderness they capture.

But again I wonder. In thirty or forty years, will wilderness art inspire people to explore, experience, and protect America's wildernesses, as was the goal of the Romantics? Not if the present trend toward a disconnection with nature continues unabated.

The destiny of America's wildernesses—as well as the health and sustainability of our air, water, and soil—has been embroiled in controversy and legal battles for nearly a half century. Past battles have resulted in some notable victories and some heartbreaking failures. I believe a powerful voice has been missing in this battle, one that could have a dramatic influence on the fate of America's remaining wild lands and on the health and sustainability of our natural environments and resources. What's been missing is God's perspective on nature and His decree that the human family be His stewards over creation. To put it more specifically, what's been missing is the Christian church.

In the following chapters, we'll learn that God permitted the human race to use nature for our own purposes, but with the understanding that nature belongs to Him and people are His caretakers. People *do not* have carte blanche to use nature for their own consumption without any regard for the environment and wild creatures. Sadly, even though this truth is clearly taught in Scriptures, Christians have generally been reluctant to get involved in confronting environmental issues. Consequently, it was secular activists, educators, and organizations that alerted the country to environmental degradation and became the vanguard of the environmental movement that emerged in the mid-1960s.

In terms of stemming the tide of environmental and ecological degradation, was this movement—propelled largely by secular environmentalists—a success or failure? And if a failure, why? Would the environmental movement have been more successful if embraced by the Christian community? Answering these questions is where our journey begins.

What Brought About the Environmental Movement?

Since the pilgrims, America's impact on nature has been, for the most part, a chronicle of neglect, misuse, exploitation, and deterioration.[1] Two classic examples illustrate this. Hope Ryden, in the thorough study of coyote eradication recorded in her book, *God's Dog*, presents Department of the Interior figures on the number of predators killed in federal government control programs for a *single* year in the 1960s, when such activity was government sanctioned. Body counts included:

> 89,653 coyotes [the target animal]; 20,780 lynx and bobcats (the lynx is endangered in the Western states); 2,779 wolves (the red wolf is endangered); 19,052 skunks; 24,273 foxes (the kit fox is endangered); 10,078 raccoons; 1,115 opossums; 6,941 badgers; 842 bears . . . [the grizzly is threatened in the lower 48 states, except Yellowstone National Park]; 294 mountain lions; and untold numbers of eagles and other rare and endangered birds. This tragic toll does not take into account the large number of poisoned animals that were never found.[2]

Although the federal government no longer sponsors such wasteful slaughter of animals, attacks on predators persist today, with the same sad results. Coyote-hunting "tournaments" were held in Nevada, Oregon, and Idaho early in 2010 to "help protect livestock." In Nevada, hunters paid a thirty-dollar entrance fee, with the entire pot going to the team that "bagged" the most coyotes over two days. The expected kill was "up to 60 coyotes."[3]

The willful and often unnecessary slaughter of predators in order to protect domestic stock and "game" animals (animals killed in recreational hunting) has had catastrophic effects on entire ecosystems. This points to a second example of America's chronic despoiling of nature.

The Kaibab game preserve on the north rim of the Grand Canyon was established in 1906. Some 20,000 sheep and cattle were introduced to share the forage with an estimated 4,000 deer. To protect the livestock and game animals, predator control efforts eradicated more than 6,000 large predators (wolves, mountain lions, coyotes, bobcats, and golden eagles). In two decades, the deer population increased to 100,000, destroying virtually all the available forage in the preserve. Tens of thousands of deer (90 percent of them) eventually starved to death—an estimated 60,000 in 1924 alone—and the range was ruined for decades.[4]

In spite of ecological calamities like the Kaibab debacle—and the slaughter of countless thousands of America's wildlife for vested interest groups—the "environmental crisis," as it came to be called, did not come into *popular* focus until the 1960s. Many conservationists and environmentalists credit the publication of biologist Rachel Carson's *Silent Spring* in 1962 as the kick-off for the modern environmental movement. Carson persuasively argued that mounting evidence indicated that man-made pollutants, in particular synthetic pesticides, were threatening the survival of large birds such as eagles, peregrine falcons, ospreys, brown pelicans, and other wildlife. Pesticide sprays were contaminating the land, and irrigation drainage from pesticide-treated crops were poisoning lakes and rivers. Carson's book was a shock to Americans who heretofore were ignorant of humanity's destructive impact on nature, and it raised concern about the negative effects of other human activities on the environment. After *Silent Spring,* hundreds of books, articles, and newspaper exposés were written to further document the rapid degradation of the natural world at the hands of Homo sapiens—as well as to promote a greater awareness and appreciation of nature.

The result was that during the 1960s and 1970s important environmental laws were enacted, including the Clean Air Act in 1963, the Wilderness Act in 1964, the Clean Water Act in 1972, the Endangered Species Act in 1973, and some two dozen other separate pieces of environmental legislature. In 1970, President Richard M. Nixon used his administrative powers to create the Environmental Protection Agency (EPA). The purposes of the EPA and environmental laws were to control industrial and automotive emissions, protect threatened and endangered wildlife, set aside wilderness areas, clean up hazardous waste, and encourage the recycling and conservation of non-renewable resources. Growing public awareness of the deteriorating state of America's natural environment gained popular momentum with "Earth Day," April 22, 1970. In sum, the environmental movement of the late 1960s and the 1970s opened America's eyes to the fact that it could no longer sustain a take-what-you-want-and-use-it-as-you-please approach to nature. It became clear that humanity was "dirtying its nest."

The environmental movement was not just about conserving natural resources, establishing wilderness areas, and curtailing pollution. It also put forward a new image of Homo sapiens' place in the "intricate web of life" by raising public awareness of our inescapable interdependence with all other life forms. The science of ecology became popular, helping people to realize that what threatens our fellow creatures on earth ultimately threatens us. After all, ecologists pointed out, Homo sapiens breathe oxygen produced from plant life—the same as insects, fish, birds, reptiles, and mammals. We get our nutrition via the food chain—the same as ants, squirrels, and coyotes. We build our dwellings from materials supplied by the earth—the same as mud-daubers, birds, and beavers. We drink water purified by an incredibly complex hydraulic system run by the sun—the same as cattle, elephants, and otters. When people disrupt and damage the ecological balance of nature through pollution, habitat destruction, or the slaughter of wildlife, it diminishes the health and quality of life not only for non-humans but also for people.

Why Did the Environmental Movement Fizzle?

There was great optimism and hope in the 1970s (sometimes referred to as the "environmental decade") that the human race would make an ecological worldview shift away from destructive exploitation and toward a relationship with the land that curtailed pollution, extinction, and the destruction of wild habitats solely for profit. Unfortunately, with the exception of some improvements in air and water quality, this didn't materialize. In spite of public zeal for environmental reform, a vocal army of professional and lay environmentalists, and tough new environmental laws, the environmental movement failed to stem the tide of environmental degradation, especially when measured on a worldwide scale. I believe there were three interconnected reasons for this.

Loss of Popular Focus

It was no coincidence that the environmental movement of the late 1960s and the 1970s paralleled the countercultural movement of the same era. Many of America's youth were fed up with the stress, smog, and congestion of city life. Those of us who entered adulthood during the 1960s felt isolated from the land. We viewed nature's plight as the fallout of rampant materialism and rapid suburbanization. The environmental movement fit like a glove with the 1960s popular rebellion against conventional values.

Historically, in American culture, when a forward-looking movement of any kind exists at a popular level, things get done. Think of John F. Kennedy's commitment in 1961 to land a man on the moon within a decade; it only took eight years. Consider Martin Luther King Jr.'s hugely popular civil rights marches in the 1960s. Think of the Vietnam War protests that erupted in universities across the country in the late 1960s. Nothing is more newsworthy than a united, popular display of dissatisfaction. The squeaky wheel gets the grease.

The environmental movement was essentially a grassroots movement. It had the same kind of broad support among the rank-and-file that these other popular movements enjoyed, especially with the emerging baby boomer generation. This zeal for nature had an interesting side effect that paralleled and, in fact, was part of the environmental movement. It spawned a back-to-the-land migration during the early 1970s. Dissatisfied with city life, more than a million people in America migrated to rural settings. By the mid-1970s, for the first time in 150 years, rural areas grew faster, proportionately, than cities.[5]

As a sociocultural phenomenon, however, the back-to-the-land movement was short lived. As one researcher put it, the "city-to-small-town movement proved to be a demographic blip. . . . The city-to-rural migration of the 1970s did not last."[6] The fading zeal to live a natural, simple, semi-isolated life on the land coincided with a loss of vigor for the environmental movement. As the 1980s moved toward the 1990s, the environmental movement increasingly lost steam. As columnist and environmental advocate Richard Louv observed, "The American conservationist may be an endangered species, both in numbers and public influence."[7]

By the 1990s, the environmental movement had all but vanished from the public eye. John Denver (1943–1997) and other folk artists no longer serenaded wild nature and encouraged people to love and protect wildlife. Films like the *Wilderness Family* movies, which romanticized living off the land in the wilderness, became a thing of the past. There was no longer an exodus of young people to rural communities and communal farms. Today's technocrats and urbanites find such notions quaint and archaic.

Although environmental activism is still popular in American universities, the environmental movement itself has evolved from a grassroots movement to the vocation of professionals and politicians. Citizen-supported environmental organizations such as the Sierra Club, National Wildlife Federation, Defenders of Wildlife, and the Wilderness Society provide organized lobbies for environmentalists. In addition, with dozens of environmental laws now in place, environmentalists can rely more on governmental action to take care of environmental problems. Litigation, ballot initiatives, environmental impact statements, and the EPA have depersonalized the environmental movement. Ironically, the goals that the environmental movement worked so passionately to achieve—establishing laws against pollution and setting aside land for wilderness and wildlife preservation—were a major contributor to its demise because of the loss of grassroots involvement.

A Nature-Starved Generation

A second reason the passion and fervor of the environmental movement waned at a popular level is that a new generation has arisen that is less interested in experiencing nature firsthand.[8] After fifty years of steady increase, attendance at various U.S. National Parks has declined between 18 and 25 percent since 1987, according to an article from *Proceedings of the National Academy of Sciences*.[9] The present generation is more sedentary and attuned to indoor activities, technological toys, cyberspace, and MTV (the report uses the term "videophilia"). The Academy of Sciences report concluded that "all major lines of evidence point to a general and fundamental shift away from people's participation in nature-based recreation."[10]

Richard Louv's *Last Child in the Woods* thoroughly documents how children today have all but lost physical contact with nature. He noted that "in the space of a century, the American experience of nature has gone from direct utilitarianism to romantic attachment to electronic detachment. . . . Americans born between 1946 and 1964 . . . may constitute the last generation of Americans to share an intimate, familial attachment to the land and water."[11] Louv further observed, "We are no longer talking about retreating to rural communes, but, rather, about building technologically and ethically sophisticated human-scale population centers that, by their design, reconnect both children and adults to nature."[12] In other words, people still want contact with nature, but they don't want to live in isolation. They want a tamed nature, a nature easily accessible and adapted to human comforts.

This change came with a cost. Louv coined the phrase "nature-deficit disorder" to describe the physical and emotional health problems that isolation from nature has created: "As one scientist puts it," Louv explained, "we can now assume that just as children need good nutrition and adequate sleep, they may very well need contact with nature. . . . A widening circle of researchers believes that the loss of natural habitats, or the disconnection from nature even when it is available, has enormous implications for human health and child development."[13] Conversely, studies have shown that illnesses such as childhood obesity, stress, and Attention Deficit Hyperactivity Disorder (ADHD) can sometimes be alleviated through physical interaction with nature.[14]

Of course all people can benefit from contact with outdoor activities. New research from England's University of Essex reports on "the positive effects of nature on human mental health." In particular, "green exercise" —such as walking or cycling in natural settings—and other contact with nature "improves psychological health by reducing stress levels, enhancing mood and self-esteem and offering a restorative environment which enables people to relax, unwind and recharge their batteries."[15]

Other researchers have expressed similar concerns over American children's loss of connectedness with nature. Conservationist and scholar Gary Paul Nabhan reports that a major reason children today lack knowledge about the natural world is that they spend more time watching television than playing outdoors, collecting rocks and insects, and exploring natural surroundings. "The vast majority of the children we interviewed," explained Nabhan, "are now gaining most of their knowledge about other organisms vicariously; 77 percent of the Mexican children, 61 percent of the Anglo children, 60 percent of the Yaqui children, and 35 percent of the O'odham children [the latter two are Native Americans] told us they had seen more animals on television and in the movies than they had personally seen in the wild." This lack of contact with nature, Nabhan continues, "will become the norm as more than 38 percent of the children born after the year 2000 are destined to live in cities with more than a million other inhabitants."[16]

Sadly, in terms of the demise of the environmental movement, the loss of connectedness with nature and the outdoors has translated into an inadvertent apathy toward the natural world. Nabhan was right when he concluded, "Because only a small percentage of humankind has any direct, daily engagement with other species of animals and plants in their habitats, we have arrived at a new era in which ecological illiteracy is the norm."[17]

For people under the age of thirty-five or forty, congestion, urbanization, and isolation from nature is like water to a fish. It's the world they grew up in; it's what they swim around in every day. Without "knowing" nature, that is, without experiencing nature on a personal level (hiking, camping, bird watching, and so on)—and passing on this joy to succeeding generations—people are easily blinded to the threats against nature that still exist, and in many cases are increasing.

The National Academy of Sciences report confirmed this. Referencing other studies, it explained,

> Human cultural learning and experience . . . [exerts] a fundamental shaping influence on the content, direction, and strength of people's nature-related values. Similarly, it has been found that environmentally responsible behavior results from direct contact with the environment and that people must be exposed to natural areas as children if they are to care about them as adults. Extended periods spent in natural areas, as well as creating a role model, seem to create the most environmentally responsible behavior and increase involvement in biodiversity conservation. Moreover, as today's adult role models spend less time in nature, this generation of children is also likely to follow suit.[18]

When I think back on my own childhood growing up in the 1950s and early 1960s, this loss of connectedness with nature is hard to imagine. I remember well the adventures and excitement of exploring the farmlands and chaparral foothills surrounding my California neighborhoods and of hikes and camping trips in forest and desert. Kids today have no idea what they're missing.

Lack of Ethical Foundation

There is one other reason why the environmental movement fizzled at a popular level, and I believe it's the major reason. It failed to generate an ethical foundation necessary to institutionalize environmental ethics in American culture. For the emerging values of the environmental movement to have become entrenched in America's corporate conscience and passed on to succeeding generations, they needed to be inculcated into society's cultural heritage. With one notable exception, this just didn't happen. The one instance in which it did happen, however, proves that it *is* possible to change an entire society's attitude toward an environmental issue and elicit willing cooperation for solutions.

In 1961, Keep America Beautiful in cooperation with the Ad Council (a public service advertising organization that focuses on social issues) created a campaign to raise public awareness of litter and other forms of pollution. Their goal was to change negative attitudes and behaviors that resulted in these activities. In the case of litter, it was a tremendous success. By the end of the campaign, "local teams had helped to reduce litter by as much as 88 percent in 300 communities, 38 states, and several countries."[19] To this day, most Americans automatically use public trash receptacles and are infuriated when they see someone throw trash out their car window. The success of the Keep America Beautiful campaign demonstrates that it is possible to create ethical norms that foster workable solutions for serious environmental problems through public cooperation.

In spite of the success of the anti-litter campaign, the fact remains that an objective foundation for environmental ethics has yet to be established in American society. There are no broad-based ethical standards by which preemptive environmental strategies can be formulated or even by which existing environmental problems can be identified with any amount of general agreement. Thus we have the ongoing debate and hostility over virtually every environmental issue that surfaces: between left and right leaning politicians, between developers and preservationists, between the EPA and environmental organizations, and so on.

I believe the only successful basis for a foundation of environmental ethics is biblical Christianity, and I'll develop this fully in later chapters.

How Do We Get Past Christian Reluctance?

In recent years there has been a resurgence of interest in environmentalism within Christendom. Sadly, however, many evangelicals have been reluctant to embrace it. The primary reason, claims Christian environmental scientist Richard T. Wright, is that "Christian antienvironmentalism is a direct consequence of political commitments. . . . People who are conservative in their religious views are very often conservative in their politics. They are often reluctant to side with groups that are perceived as being more liberal, usually pro-Democratic Party, as the environmental organizations often are."[20] Christian environmental writer Michael S. Northcott adds that "many conservative Christians in the United States regard environmentalism as both a betrayal of the American dream of liberty and prosperity, and a pagan subversion of true, biblical Christianity."[21]

I agree that the reluctance of many evangelicals to wholeheartedly embrace environmentalism is often political and ideological in nature. However, I would add that there is another reason for the lack of Christian involvement in ecological and environmental issues. Environmental stewardship does not jump out of the pages of Scripture, as do other social concerns. The New Testament in particular focuses primarily on spiritual and moral issues: the person and work of Jesus Christ, struggles with sin and temptation, how to be reconciled to God, church and family relationships, and moral issues. As a result, many Christians have historically failed to recognize the host of verses and passages woven throughout the Bible, especially in the Old Testament (which is part of Christian Scriptures) that have a strong ecological and environmental emphasis.

New Testament professor at the University of Aberdeen, Scotland, I. Howard Marshall makes an important observation relevant to this. He points out that other social problems were not recognized or widely acknowledged by past generations of Christians (and society at large) but they later burdened the conscience of the church, such as slavery, the horrid conditions under which children often worked, and prohibiting women from voting. In a similar way, explains professor Marshall, "The problems of the environment [were], by and large, not part of ancient thinking. After all, the environment hardly constituted a problem, in view of the comparative smallness of the world's population at that time and of its limited capacity to plunder or destroy nature. In no way could there have been a consciousness of the problem that we now have, which is so largely the result of the behavior of sinful people."[22]

We shouldn't be surprised that environmental ethics and stewardship were not on the church's agenda until recently. Environmental exploitation and the deterioration of natural environments were not recognized as a problem until the mid-twentieth century—just as slavery and child labor practices were not recognized as unbiblical until the nineteenth century. What is regrettable is that as the seriousness of the environmental crisis became widely acknowledged, more Christians did not get involved in the environmental movement. God instructed the human race to be His stewards over nature, and the Bible reveals moral principles on which to develop environmental ethics and guidelines for environmental stewardship. The church should have been the vanguard of the environmental movement.

Be that as it may, the church failed to develop an environmental ethos because it never developed a theology of nature leading to a precise environmental doctrine. We'll look at the primary reason for this in the following chapter. The point for now is that, as a *secular* phenomenon, the modern environmental movement was unsuccessful in terms of establishing environmental ethics in popular culture. Nor, by the way, were such ethics established through the passage of environmental laws. Without an ethical base, the environmental movement was unable to sustain the momentum it had in the 1970s and early 1980s, especially for a new generation of mostly indoor people.

❖   ❖

Would an environmental movement within the Christian community have had more success than the secular environmental movement of the 1970s and 1980s? If God-centered, I believe it would. In later chapters, I'll build a case for Bible-based environmental ethics and stewardship and suggest practical guidelines for implementing both in the Christian community. I'll also give suggestions on how the church—and individual Christians—can become godly advocates and participants in ecological activities. But first, several preliminary issues must be examined.

To begin with, Christians must confront an image problem. As a world-and-life view, Christianity has been targeted by many environmentalists as the "root cause" of today's environmental and ecological problems. The fallout from this has been that spiritually-minded non-Christian environmentalists are turning to other religions as a source of moral and spiritual guidance in environmental activism (the subject of chapter 3). Refuting the erroneous assumption that environmental degradation is directly related to the growth and spread of Christianity is the topic of the next chapter.

CHAPTER TWO

ARE CHRISTIANS RESPONSIBLE FOR THE ENVIRONMENTAL CRISIS?

When it comes to finger pointing, virtually every non-Christian environmentalist agrees on one hypothesis: The origin of today's environmental crisis can be traced directly to the Christian worldview. The most well-known and widely quoted advocate of this theory was the late historian Lynn White Jr. In an address to the American Association for the Advancement of Science in 1966, White presented his thesis that the historical source of the present "ecological crisis" was Western culture's Judeo-Christian tradition, in particular its doctrine of creation. His influential lecture was later published in *Science*, "The Historical Roots of Our Ecologic Crisis,"[1] and reprinted and anthologized numerous times in scholarly journals and popular publications.

White traced the modern environmental crisis to the marriage of science and technology under the umbrella of Christianity in the middle of the nineteenth century. Although other cultures developed technology, White pointed out that "both modern technology and modern science are distinctively *Occidental*" (Western).[2] His basic premise was that "orthodox Christian arrogance toward nature" arose from the biblical teaching that man was made in God's image and thus shares God's transcendence over nature. This was demonstrated, White believed, when God allowed man to "name all the animals, thus establishing his dominance over them."[3] Consequently, according to White's theology, Christians believe that nature was created for mankind's personal use—it was designed to serve the human race. Empowered by a divine right to dominate nature, Christians felt justified to indiscriminately exploit nature with little regard for the consequences. The result was that Christianity, especially in its Western form, became "the most anthropocentric religion the world has seen."[4]

Because White believed that the origin of the environmental crisis was rooted in Christian religious beliefs, he maintained that the solution does not lie with technology but with a change of religion: "More science and more technology are not going to get us out of the present ecologic crisis until we find a new religion, or rethink our old one."[5] White suggested that some non-Christian religions advanced a more ethical attitude toward nature than Christianity. He hinted that Eastern or animistic religions were possible alternatives. For example, cultures practicing animism believe that nature is imbued with spiritual forces. Supposedly, this compels them to revere nature and to live in ecological harmony with the natural world (more on this in chapter 3). Christianity, on the other hand, having desacralized nature, exploited it with "indifference to the feelings of natural objects."[6] Thus, White asserted, "the victory of Christianity over paganism was the greatest psychic revolution in the history of culture."[7] In other words, by abolishing the spiritual forces that pagan animists associated with nature, Christianity opened the door for Western societies to degrade and exploit the natural environment with little concern for the land and the welfare of nonhuman life.

During the 1970s and early 1980s (the halcyon days of the environmental movement), many environmental writers joined Lynn White Jr. in blaming Christianity for the present environmental crisis. Environmental historian Donald Worster, in his well-researched history of ecology, *Nature's Economy,* stated: "Christianity has maintained a calculated indifference, if not antagonism, toward nature. The good shepherd, the heroic benefactor of man, has almost never been concerned with leading his flock to a broad reverence for life."[8]

Bolen and Robinson's textbook, *Wildlife Ecology and Management,* used in university history of wildlife conservation classes, claimed that "the underlying attitude expressed in Genesis that portrays the earth as the dominion of man . . . has influenced the behavior of hundreds of generations [*sic*] of humans who have lived in western Asia, Europe, and more recently in the Western Hemisphere. . . . Of the instructions to Adam and Eve, the one taken most seriously by western man was to subdue the earth."[9]

Controversial Princeton University professor Peter Singer, in his 1975 book on animal rights, *Animal Liberation*, left no doubts about his view when he stated,

> The biblical story of the creation sets out very clearly the nature of the relationship between man and animal as the Hebrew people conceived it to be. . . .
>
> The Bible tells us that God made man in His own image. We may regard this as man making God in his own image. Either way, it allots man a special position in the universe, as a being that, alone of all living things, is God-like. Moreover, God is explicitly said to have given man dominion over every living thing. . . .
>
> Christianity spread the idea that every human life—and only human life—is sacred. . . .
>
> The New Testament is completely lacking in any injunction against cruelty to animals, or any recommendation to consider their interests. Jesus himself showed indifference to the fate of nonhumans.[10]

The eminent French zoologist, Jean Dorst (1924–2001), suggested that Eastern philosophies reflect a greater respect for non-human life than Western religions. He stated in his book *Before Nature Dies* that Western "philosophies emphasize the supremacy of man over the rest of creation, which exists only to serve him."[11] He substantiated this claim by quoting Genesis 1:28–29.

Environmental scientist Jeremy Rifkin in his popular book, *Entropy: A New World View*, commented, "The traditional Christian approach to nature has been a major contributing factor to ecological destruction. The overemphasis on otherworldliness has led to disregard and even exploitation of the physical world."[12]

The question these books raise, however, is not whether their opinions are believed but whether they're true. As philosophy professor Robin Attfield pointed out, "Even if the Bible is not despotic as to its writers' view of nature . . . the teaching of its adherents could still have been so."[13]

Attfield's point is important because it's true. There has been a disparity between what the Bible teaches with regard to mankind's responsibilities in creation and how Christians have behaved toward nature. It saddens me to admit it, but throughout church history the majority of Christians have exercised a destructive exploitive attitude toward nature. However—and this is a crucial point—*all* cultures and societies, past or present and regardless of religious beliefs, have likewise exploited their natural environments. This being the case, Christianity is not the cause of today's environmental crisis—the entire human race is guilty.

Who Is to Blame for the Environmental Crisis?

Since Eden the entire human race has done irreparable damage to nature and the land. Early societies negatively impacted their environment thousands of years before industrialization. The history of the human race, following Adam and Eve's expulsion from the Garden of Eden, reveals a steady increase in environmental exploitation that has transformed large tracts of pristine wilderness into blighted wasteland. Jean Dorst documented the widespread environmental degradation that occurred over many parts of the ancient world centuries before the arrival of Europeans, including North America, Africa, Asia, the Mid East, and Australia.[14]

Dorst's chronology begins with primitive hunting and gathering societies. Tribal cultures purposely destroyed vast areas of wilderness with fire in order to enlarge hunting areas. This, along with hunting itself, likely hastened the extinction of the mammoth, mastodon, cave bear, and ground sloth.

Several thousand years before God instructed Abram (Abraham) to set out for the land of Canaan (Gen. 12:1–5), hunting and gathering began to decline and the human race turned increasingly to herding sheep, goats, and (eventually) other livestock. Like hunters and gatherers, herders also burned brush and forests, although in their case the purpose was to create better forage for livestock. In the process, however, they not only destroyed native plants and eliminated forest dwelling wildlife, but they also overgrazed the land, creating habitats vulnerable to erosion. The result was that vast areas around the world, particularly in the Mediterranean region and Near East, were destroyed long before industrial civilization.

Farmers followed the herders, and damaged native environments far more extensively. In particular, primitive agriculture practices caused widespread deforestation, soil depletion, and erosion. Heavily forested areas in central and northern Europe were destroyed three to four thousand years before Christ. In Africa, where forest originally covered most of the continent, major environmental devastation began in prehistoric times. "The transformation of Africa," explained Dorst, "shows that primitive man could leave his mark on an entire continent long before he had powerful tools at his disposal."[15] Nor were tropical regions in the New World immune to environmental degradation. The disappearance of the Mayan Empire, "one of the most highly developed [civilizations] in Central America was chiefly caused by deforestation, shifting cultivation . . . and fires that were set to transform habitats."[16]

In short, Dorst and other researchers[17] have unarguably demonstrated that non-Western, non-Christian, and non-technological people have poor environmental track records. Environmental degradation through burning native foliage, overgrazing, erosion, pollution, and the extermination of plant and animal species has been widespread throughout human history—and began thousands of years before the Christian era. If the human race is more destructive today than past generations, it's because more people inhabit the earth and have at their disposal greater technological tools for environmental exploitation. This sheds light on the true origin of today's environmental crisis.

The Scientific and Industrial Revolutions

Long before the twentieth century's environmental crisis, factors outside the purview of Christianity exploded across the Western world and were ultimately responsible for future damaging environmental exploitation and degradation. In particular, the root cause of today's environmental crisis was technology running amok without ethical restraints. This began with the scientific and industrial revolutions.

The change from an agrarian economy to one dominated by industry and machines brought about sweeping economic, political, and social changes. The scientific and industrial revolutions resulted in unchecked technological power over nature and created environmental pollution and degradation as we know it today. It was not Christianity that caused this, but unbridled technology operating within an emerging secular society.

To keep this in proper context, it should be understood that after the Enlightenment, the rise of modern science and advances in highly efficient technology occurred simultaneously with the fading authority and influence of the Christian worldview. As French historian and sociologist Jacques Ellul stated, "The technical movement of the West developed in a world which had already withdrawn from the dominant influence of Christianity."[18]

Prior to the eighteenth century Enlightenment, the majority of scientists (including those who birthed the scientific revolution—Bacon, Copernicus, Kepler, Newton, and Galileo, to name a few) were Christians who believed God created the universe and mankind and that the Bible provided a general foundation of natural history. Scientists and theologians were partners seeking insight and understanding into God and His creation. As Enlightenment scholar Peter Gay stated, the purpose of medieval science "was knowledge for the sake of God; and its discoveries were discoveries of purposes—God's intentions for His creation."[19] "In fact," wrote the late theologian Langdon Gilkey, "right up to the end of the eighteenth century, it was taken for granted that Biblical truth included all manner of statement about the age and early stages of the world's geological life, the creation of plants and animals, the making and early history of man, important facts of relevant geography—as well as trustworthy statements about the sacred history on which our redemption depended."[20]

The mutually beneficial relationship between science and Christianity began to change dramatically during and following the eighteenth century Enlightenment. From that period on, Christianity was being shoved off center stage as the dominant worldview in Western culture, and humanity was replacing God as Supreme Being. This reached fruition in the nineteenth century with the publication of Charles Darwin's *Origin of Species* (which provided an explanation for the origin of life without God) and the rise of higher biblical criticism (which jettisoned the infallibility of Scripture, thereby removing its authority). Together, these views were the icing on the secular cake and resulted in the liberalization of America's mainline churches and the demise of the Christian worldview as the guiding moral light in Western culture.[21]

By the twentieth century, humanists openly challenged God's existence, and science was considered throughout academia as the only criterion for determining truth. The view that nature was a signature of God's general revelation and an expression of His power and glory virtually disappeared in the scientific community. Thus, by the beginning of the modern environmental crisis in the mid-twentieth century, Christianity was no longer the dominant worldview in the West, and the authority of Scripture outside the church had been largely rejected in popular culture. During the interim between the end of the Christian era and the modern environmental crisis, no ethical constraints arose to control—let alone prevent—the crushing technological exploitation of the earth's natural environments.

❖   ❖

In sum, Christianity did not drive environmental exploitation; the human race did, through its use of unregulated technology.

Perhaps, had the church developed an environmental ethos, it could have mitigated the damage wrought by unrestrained technology. However, the fact that by the end of the nineteenth century Christianity had lost much of its authority and influence in Western societies, plus the unjustified assumption by critics such as Lynn White Jr. that it was responsible for today's environmental crisis, removed virtually any hope that the Western world would turn to biblical Christianity when the modern environmental crisis arose. As a result, in recent years, many non-Christians have suggested that other religious traditions are more ecologically and environmentally responsible than Christianity and should be sought for guidance in environmental ethics and stewardship. We will explore this argument in the next chapter.

CHAPTER THREE

ARE NON-CHRISTIAN RELIGIONS MORE ENVIRONMENTALLY RESPONSIBLE THAN CHRISTIANITY?

In the early 1970s, my wife and I became enthusiastic supporters of the American Indian Movement (AIM) that began in 1968. We read books on Native American cultures and collected Indian pottery and other artifacts. We traveled extensively throughout the Navajo, Hopi, and other reservations, visiting places now off limits to the public. To show our support for AIM's goal of economic independence, autonomy, and the restoration of "illegally" seized lands, we placed a bumper sticker on our 1973 Volkswagen camper that had a drawing of an Indian head nickel followed by the words, "The only Indian America ever loved."

Like many young people during the heyday of the environmental movement (the 1970s), my wife and I believed that Native American cultures exhibited a genuine kinship with plants and animals and a true reverence for "Mother Earth." To us, they epitomized living in ecological harmony with nature. It was no coincidence that our growing interest in Native American cultures during the early days of the environmental movement paralleled our growing ecological awareness. It was widely assumed among environmentalists during that era that Native Americans' reverence for nature was a direct result of their religious beliefs and practices.

But is this true? Let's examine this issue closely.

Religion and Ethics

Moral behavior is primarily—if not always—linked to religious beliefs. It's not surprising, therefore, that people who are concerned about the environment, such as the late Lynn White Jr., recognize the need for a spiritual foundation for environmental ethics and stewardship. In Western culture, ethical standards are rooted in the Judeo-Christian worldview. Nevertheless, from the beginning of the modern environmental movement and as people began to search for spiritual guidance in environmental matters, few considered biblical Christianity. We learned in chapter 2 that this was because most environmentalists assume that Christianity is ecologically bankrupt and is the source of Western culture's destructive, exploitive behavior. More often than not, environmentally-minded spiritual seekers turn to Eastern and tribal religions (animism) for guidance in environmental stewardship rather than Christianity. Christian environmental writer Ghillean T. Prance issued a warning about this:

> There is obviously a growing realization in the secular world that the environmental crisis is indeed a moral issue, and so the world is turning to religious leaders and philosophers for help. This is a challenge to which Christians must be in the forefront of the response if there is to be any lasting and serious commitment to responsible, sustainable stewardship of our planet. If we do not respond, our place will be taken by false gods and other religions that worship creation rather than the Creator.[1]

Popular Christian writer Tony Campolo put it even more sternly:

> If we fail to develop a *biblically based* theology of nature that fosters feelings for nature, then other religions and New Age gurus will move in to offer alternative belief systems that do. If the church cannot teach the citizens of our century how to

enter into the suffering of creation, those false prophets who play with the occult will. Then charlatans will be the only ones to offer people a spiritual basis for being pro-actively responsible for their environment.[2]

The tendency of many environmentalists to reject Christianity and turn to Eastern and tribal religions in their quest for spiritual guidance in healing and caring for the earth raises two questions. Is it true that these two broad religious worldviews are more ecologically in tune with nature than Christianity and, as a result, they more readily embrace environmental stewardship? If so, is this a theological teaching or an unrelated side effect? I believe it's the latter, and I'll demonstrate in this chapter that any apparent ecological dimension present in Eastern and tribal religions is actually a by-product—not doctrine. Not only have non-Christian religions failed to restrain environmental degradation in their own cultures (as demonstrated in chapter 2), but also they have no explicit theological teachings that the human race should protect and care for nature because it has value independent of humanity—or because a deity instructed them to do so.

Tribal Societies

Today, many people have a romanticized, Hollywood-tainted image of pre-Columbian cultures. They visualize early American Indians, Australian Aborigines, and native Africans as living in a harmonious, ecologically sensitive relationship with nature. After all, hunting deer and buffalo and gathering wild vegetables and roots were methods of sustenance similar to that of wild animals. Such food gathering did not upset the balance of nature. Native peoples were assumed to have taken from the land only what they needed and no more. Pollution was not a problem because no one used synthetic pesticides and fertilizers. Bodily waste was naturally recycled in the ecosystem. A simple thatched hut or teepee required few natural resources. A small fire used little fuel. Walking left only footprints. In sum, the popular image of pre-Columbian cultures is that people enjoyed a lifestyle that had little negative impact on nature.

There is a reason that Native American and other preliterary tribal cultures throughout the world appear to have been more environmentally friendly than Western societies. For thousands of years, their way of life was closely tied to the land, and survival depended entirely on a successful relationship with the natural world. As a result, native peoples developed a remarkable knowledge of their physical environments, and their cultural identity became inseparable from nature and the land.

It is often taken for granted that the apparent ecological consciousness observed in preliterary tribal societies was directly related to their religious beliefs. It's assumed, for example, that Native Americans "embraced conservation, ecology, and environmentalism . . . [based] on a spiritual, sacred attitude toward land and animals, not a practical utilitarian one."[3] For this reason, many environmentalists have suggested that Westerners turn to Native American cultures for insight into environmental ethics and guidance in environmental stewardship.

A widely read book that promulgated Native Americans' alleged ecologically sensitive relationship with nature is T. C. McLuhan's *Touch the Earth*, which is a collection of speeches and writings by Native Americans from the sixteenth century to the twentieth century. In the introduction to his book, the author stated that the writings

> speak with courtesy and respect of the land, of animals, of the objects which made up the territory in which they live. They saw no virtue in imposing their will over the environment. . . .
>
> Many of the passages in this book represented the Indians' attempt to offer their ideas to the white man. . . .
>
> It is well understood that the only decent future for us who live in America now is through a rediscovery of our environment. We need to establish a right relationship with the land and its resources. . . .
>
> The Indian, in a sense, knew this all along. For many

generations they learned how to live in America, in a state of balance; or, as a Christian would say, in a state of grace. Perhaps now, after hundreds of years of ignoring their wisdom, we may now learn from the Indians.[4]

In reality, this respect for nature did not play out in effective conservation efforts. The so-called "Ecological Indian" is more myth than fact. Native Americans were not innocent of environmental abuse, and few tribes lived in continuous harmony with nature. Conservation scientist and professor Gary Paul Nabhan challenged the "Ecological Indian" assumption. We often hear, he observed, that

> "Before the White Man came, North America was essentially a wilderness where the few Indian inhabitants lived in constant harmony with nature"—even though four to twelve million people speaking two hundred languages variously burned, pruned, hunted, hacked, cleared, irrigated, and planted an astonishing diversity of habitats for centuries. . . . And we are supposed to believe, as well, that they all lived in some static homeostasis with all the various plants and animals they encountered.[5]

Native Americans (and other tribal cultures) often used fire to manipulate the environment for their own interests. This practice was widespread across the continent, and on the Great Plains fires could be a hundred miles across. Fires were used to drive and encircle animals so that they could be more easily killed; to create forage for animals the Indians depended on for food (or alternatively, to ruin forage and force animals into areas where they were more easily hunted); to improve pasture for horse herds; to clear land for crops; and even to "confuse, hinder, maim, or kill their enemies, Indian or white, to drive them from or into cover, or to mask their own actions."[6]

It has also been documented by archaeologists that Indian tribes in

North America engaged in massive overkill by stampeding entire bison herds over cliffs, slaying many more animals than the tribes could possibly use. Reportedly, more than a thousand bison were slaughtered in a single hunt. Nor did Indians always use every portion of the kill, as often alleged. Sometimes just the best part of the meat was taken (the tongues and humps) and the rest was left to rot. Artist and anthropologist George Catlin, who lived several years among Native Americans, recorded the following event:

> When I first arrived at this place, on my way up the river, which was in the month of May, in 1832, and had taken up my lodgings in the Fur Company's Fort, . . . [I was told] that only a few days before I arrived (when an immense herd of buffaloes had showed themselves on the opposite side of the river, almost blackening the plains for a great distance), a party of five or six hundred Sioux Indians on horseback, forded the river about mid-day, and spending a few hours among them [the buffalo], recrossed the river at sun-down and came into the Fort with *fourteen hundred fresh buffalo tongues* [emphasis his], which were thrown down in a mass [to be traded for whiskey]. . . .
>
> This profligate waste of the lives of these noble and useful animals, when, from all that I could learn, not a skin or a pound of meat (except the tongues) was brought in, fully supports me in the seemingly extravagant predictions that I have made as to their extinction, which I am certain is near at hand. . . .[7]

In recent times, Native Americans have willingly accepted the negative consequences of modern technology in order to promote economic development. On the Navajo and Hopi reservations, strip mining and power plants provide jobs, but at the expense of pollution and "deeply scarred, stripped lands [that] will take centuries to recover." Other tribes have shown an interest in becoming waste-disposal sites, even of radio-active waste.[8]

This is not said to disparage Native Americans or to deny the fact that indigenous people throughout the world, regardless of whether they are motivated by survival necessities or love of nature, typically express a deep respect for their natural surroundings. Many tribal people today express a great desire to protect the land. The question at hand is not whether tribal people exhibited a reverential and ecological sensitivity to nature, but whether those sentiments were an explicit teaching in their religious beliefs. More to the point, do tribal religions provide ethical principles and guidelines for environmental stewardship? Answering this question requires that we examine the religious beliefs of tribal societies before the influence of Christianity and Western culture.

Pre-Christian Tribal Cultures

Tribal societies before contact with Christianity are often portrayed in popular culture as virtual utopias: paradisaical societies inhabited by care-free, happy natives. Sustenance is no more difficult than scaling a coconut tree, picking breadfruit, spearing fish, or stalking abundant game with homemade weapons. Religion has the appearance of Halloween-like ceremonies consisting of bizarre but innocuous (and always fascinating) fireside chants and dances. Nature is esteemed, revered, and respected. Here in America, this belief has been proliferated by myriad books on Native American cultures and by Hollywood movies such as *Dances with Wolves*. In the animated Disney movie *Pocahontas*, the Indian maiden sings about herons and otters who are her "friends" and of the "hoop that never ends."

Do fiction books and movies accurately depict life in pre-Christian-influence tribal societies? Were religious practices gleeful occasions of social fellowship and communal worship? Did tribal people live in *spiritual* harmony with their environment, loving and venerating Mother Earth? In particular, for our purposes, do the religious beliefs of tribal cultures embrace ethical principles and guidelines that can be applied remedially to modern environmental and ecological issues?

In the mid-nineteenth century, the new science of anthropology increased American and European contact with preliterary societies. Most of these scientists (as well as explorers and other adventurers) agreed that an enormous gulf existed between civilized man and the "savage," and that the former was far superior to the latter in every way. Charles Darwin visited the coast of Tierra Del Fuego and spent several months among some of the most "impoverished people on earth." Nothing in their way of life appealed to him. Darwin wrote in his journal: "These poor wretches were stunted in their growth, their hideous faces bedaubed with white paint, their skins filthy and greasy, their hair entangled, their voices discordant, their gestures violent. . . . I could not have believed how wide was the difference between savage and civilized man: it is greater than between a wild and domesticated animal, inasmuch as in man there is greater power of improvement."[9]

The assumption that before contact with Christianity tribal people lived in an idyllic relationship with their physical and spiritual surroundings is a fairly recent and largely mythical notion. It has only been since the last century that Darwin's demeaning view was replaced by the "noble savage" image. Tribal Man became Natural Man. The truth, however, is far different from this popular sentiment. The fact is that before Christian missionaries liberated many of them, tribal cultures were in bondage to religious beliefs that were embedded in a deep-seated fear of the spiritual world—and even of their physical environments. The world of preliterary tribal societies was not friendly and innocent; it was hostile, threatening, and had to be constantly appeased.

Animism

Since the beginning of the nineteenth century, most preliterary societies have either disappeared or have been radically altered by foreign cultures. Today, probably only 6.5 to 7.5 percent of the world's population still lives in a "primitive" state.[10] Nevertheless, tribal cultures exist in Asia, Australia, New Guinea, Indonesia, Africa, the Pacific Islands, and North and South America.

The religion of all preliterary societies, including Native Americans, is collectively called *animism*. Technically, animism is not so much a distinct religion as a belief or component of many religions, including Shinto, some forms of Hinduism, and neo-paganism. In the United States, animistic beliefs are especially prevalent in New Age channeling and personal spirit guides. Nevertheless, for the purpose of classification, animism can be considered the "religion" of indigenous cultures worldwide.

Like most religions, animism embraces a multiplicity of beliefs and a variety of religious practices. Nevertheless, one fundamental doctrine is shared by all tribal cultures. It has a direct bearing on what actually motivates their reverence for nature and apparent ecological sensitivity.

The Spirit World

The Perennial Dictionary of World Religions defines animism as "The belief that all of reality is pervaded or inhabited by spirits or souls; the belief that all of reality is in some sense animate."[11] The operative word in this definition is "spirits." The fundamental doctrine of animism (and the central belief of all tribal religions) is that most (if not all) living things are endowed with spirits that have intelligence and volition identical to that of people. It's believed, for example, that many wild animals function similarly to humans. They possess emotions and have the ability to reason and speak (although they usually remain silent). In fact, many animists believe that animals often have greater power and are more cunning than people.

Spirits may also dwell in inanimate objects and natural phenomena such as rocks, lightning, rivers, lakes, caves, mountains, and countless other strategic places. As Pocahontas sang in the Disney movie of the same name, "I know every rock and tree and creature has a life, has a spirit, has a name."

Unlike in the movie *Pocahontas*, however, these spirits are not necessarily friendly. Whatever their locale, they are considered unpredictable. They may be either malevolent or benevolent, and people must be extremely careful "not to offend them and to pay proper respect [sometimes] by making small offerings of food when they pass by their supposed dwelling places."[12] Writing about Native Americans, anthropology professor Harold Driver explained:

> [Spirits] may intervene in the affairs of the world and of man in a manner consistent with a system of ethics or according to their whims of the moment. Because of their humanlike emotions, they may experience love, hate, joy, anger, jealousy, fear, courage, and may act according to their emotional state at the time. They may be benevolent, malevolent, or merely unconcerned, but they are generally susceptible to human pleading, and bend an ear to prayers, sacrifices, and other forms of emotional appeal to their egos.[13]

Although most tribal cultures acknowledge the existence of a Supreme Being, religious activities focus on the spirit world. Through sacrifices, prayers, and especially rituals, tribal people hope to appease the host of spirits that lurk throughout nature. The purpose of these activities is not to praise the spirits or nature itself, but to ward off evil such as sickness and barrenness of wives, and to enlist the aid of spiritual forces to help the tribe enjoy the good things in life: many children, successful hunting, plenty of food, wealth, respect, and long life.

The belief that a potentially hostile spirit world permeates all of nature is key to understanding the motivation behind many nature-honoring rituals—and tribal societies' apparent reverence for nature. It turns out that this "reverence" is based more on fear than veneration.

Fear of Nature

Contrary to the claims of many environmentalists (and Hollywood), tribal people regard nature with a combination of awe, reverence, and dread. The authors of *Understanding Folk Religions* wrote: "A final worldview theme that runs through nearly all folk religious belief systems is near constant fear and the need for security. In a world full of spirits, witchcraft, sorcery, black magic, curses, bad omens, broken taboos, angry ancestors, human enemies, and false accusations of many kinds, life is rarely carefree and secure."[14] Former missionary Edward Newing agreed: "There is no doubt that the world of the PLS [preliterary society] is a fearful one. Fear plays an important role in life."[15]

So, on the one hand, tribal cultures possess a sense of kinship, respect, dependence, and gratitude toward their natural environments. On the other hand, every event in life—health, safety, marriage, childbirth, hunting, sowing, and building—is potentially at the mercy of harmful spiritual forces that must be appeased: "All face the threat of failure, barrenness, disease, drought, floods, fires, and a thousand other misfortunes that plague human life."[16]

Although religious beliefs and practices observed in tribal cultures are closely bound to nature, revering nature for nature's sake is not their intent. Any apparent concern for nature's welfare arising out of tribal religions is a *side effect*, a by-product, and not doctrine. Ecological sensitivity is incidental to acts of appeasement toward a hostile spiritual world. It is not due to a benevolent relationship among deity, humans, and nature.

This is not to say that tribal people cannot feel a sense of wonder, awe, and reverence toward nature alongside of religious beliefs. Of course they can, just the same as any other human being. Moreover, many tribal people today have a genuine, heartfelt desire to live in harmony with nature and promote environmental stewardship. But such reverence and desire are without a theological framework. Animism contains no religious principles or doctrines that give specific instructions on environmental stewardship.

If modern environmentalists turn to tribal religions for moral principles on which to develop environmental ethics and for guidance in environmental stewardship, they will be bonding with religious beliefs that are historically grounded in fear and in the desire to manipulate nature to benefit people.

Eastern Religions

In addition to tribal religions, many people concerned about the environment believe that Eastern religions are more environmentally sensitive than Christianity. Religion professors Denise and John Carmody are typical:

> The biblical and traditional Jewish views do not encourage the pollution of nature, but they open the door to such abuse (as do the Christian and Muslim views) by downplaying nature's closeness to God. All three Western traditions might learn something important from the East, where nature's closer identification with the ultimate or divine has provided the basis for a religion of great ecological sensitivity. The Eastern peoples have not fully practiced this religion (they have their own share of ecological sins), but the flowering of their deepest instincts would seem to imply treating nature very reverently, with greater friendship than the West has recognized.[17]

The term "Eastern religions" encompasses numerous religious traditions. The two most popular in the United States, both considered to be more environmentally responsible than Christianity, are Buddhism and Hinduism. Today, around three million Buddhists and one and a half million Hindus live in America.[18] Before we examine the alleged environmentally responsible teachings found in some Eastern religions, I want to remind you—as I did with animism—that Eastern religions have also failed to curb ecological abuse and exploitation among the societies that practice them. India and China, for example, have experienced devastating environmental degradation due to increased salinity and alkalinity in soil, air and water pollution, improper use of pesticides and fertilizers, erosion, flooding, desertification, and deforestation. Millions of acres of wildlife habitats have been destroyed, threatening the survival of numerous species of animals.[19] In much of the rest of Asia, and in spite of so-called ecologically sensitive Eastern religions, population pressure and a "certain contempt for nature in the wild" had already caused "irreparable damage" to the environment well before the influence of Europeans.[20] David Livingstone, professor of geosciences, commented on this:

> Deforestation and erosion, rice terracing and urbanization have all exacted an immense toll on the environment and effected a gigantic transformation of the Chinese landscape. . . . Erich Isaac speaks of the destruction wrought by Arab imperial expansionists on vast tracts of the Old World and of the devastation of central Burma by Buddhists. Such are ignored, if not suppressed, among critics of the Judeo-Christian West.[21]

Any ecological dimensions that may be present in Eastern religions have not resulted in serious efforts to control damaging environmental exploitation or to promote environmental stewardship—including countries where Buddhism and Hinduism are the dominant religious beliefs.

Pantheism

Eastern religions subscribe to a *pantheistic* concept of God. Pantheism teaches that God is an impersonal substance or essence that encompasses all of reality. "God" is everything and everything *is* God—the universe and all that exists within it. Nature is part of God's essence; God and nature do not exist independent of each other. Thus, in pantheism, God did not create nature.

Because pantheism teaches that the physical world is part of God's essential nature, it's taken for granted by some Western environmentalists that Eastern religions automatically embrace safeguards against environmental abuse. The fundamental oneness of God, humanity, and nature supposedly sensitizes people to nature's welfare; thus, it's assumed, believers in Eastern religions instinctively possess a greater willingness to care for their natural environments than Western religions.

In reality, it's more likely to be the opposite. Theologically and philosophically, pantheism should *preclude* environmental ethics and stewardship for the very reason that God and nature *are* one in essence. Let me explain.

Since the pantheistic god did not personally and of its own volition create life on earth, there is no compelling reason or ability for "It" to have any interest in nature's welfare or people, for that matter. Only a *personal,* transcendent God, one willfully active in creation, would (or could) formulate environmental ethics and hold people accountable for not obeying His ordained stewardship instructions. Furthermore, many pantheists believe that if something appears to exist independent of God, it must be an *illusion*. If observable nature is merely an illusion, why bother to care for it? In short, pantheism does not have a theological framework for environmental ethics and stewardship because it lacks a transcendent, personal, creator God.

The Eightfold Path

A second feature that appears to foster greater sensitivity toward nature in Eastern religions—in this case among Buddhists—is the Eightfold Path. Buddhism teaches that all suffering comes from cravings. If there are no cravings, there is no suffering. The way to eliminate cravings (and hence suffering) is to follow the Eightfold Path (which is the last of the so-called Four Noble Truths). The Eightfold Path is a disciplined course of self-improvement that can lead to Nirvana, the extinction of desires and individual consciousness. In this state, all earthly passions, including cravings (along with greed, hate, and other human foibles) are extinguished.

The ecological attraction of this philosophy lies in its opposition to consumption. Unlike many Westerners, who often measure success according to the quantity of things they possess, the Buddha taught his followers not to crave anything. A Buddhist desires liberation from earthly passions, including material cravings. The obvious appeal of such a philosophy, environmentally speaking, is that fewer human demands will result in less consumption of natural resources which, in turn, will result in less environmental abuse.

Although this sounds good on paper, few people in the West would consistently go along with a philosophy that rejects material possessions. Apparently, it's unlikely many people in the East will either, if they can afford to live otherwise. Witness the immense desire for automobiles and other modern conveniences in China as it has become an increasingly wealthy country.

Ahimsa

An even stronger ecological dimension common in Eastern religions is the doctrine of *ahimsa*—the law of non-violence toward all living things. *Ahimsa* has its roots in karma and the transmigration of souls. The "law" of karma is a principle of cause and effect in which one's actions in this life determine his or her fate in the next stage of existence. To westernize this concept, there will be retribution in later lives for "sins" committed in earlier lives.

Most pantheists believe that before people reach oneness with the ultimate reality (Nirvana to Buddhists and Brahman to Hindus), their eternal souls are trapped in a seemingly endless cycle of births, lives, deaths, and rebirths as dictated by the law of karma. To reach a state of bliss wherein one is set free from this cycle, people must maintain good karma. Bad karma results in a debt against the soul, negatively affecting a person's destiny either in this life or the next. Because souls can wander through every life form (human, bird, rodent, insect, etc.), all living things, even the lowliest, are respected and preserved. "No sin is greater than the taking of life, even though it be only the gnat or the worm that perishes."[22] Just harming another creature can be a serious offense: "To contribute to the further suffering of any individual member of [the animal kingdom] would be as serious an offense as harming one's mother or father."[23]

Ecologically speaking, this "sanctity" of life is assumed to result in greater compassion for the suffering of all creatures. "In Buddhist perspective we can be friends of the earth if we recognize our kinship with all fellow creatures and practice *ahimsa* (non-violence) toward them."[24]

The question, however, is not whether some Eastern religions instruct followers to avoid harming other creatures, but whether this aversion is a theological teaching designed to protect animals *independent* of human self-interest—a characteristic of true environmental stewardship.[25] The answer to this question is no. The desire to avoid harming animals does not flow from a religious doctrine that teaches altruism toward other living things. Rather, it is totally human-centered. In other words, a Hindu's apprehension over harming animals is not about protecting creatures because they are of value in their own right or because it honors and pleases God. Rather the motivation driving *ahimsa* is to maintain good karma. Harming other creatures can result in bad karma. This negatively impacts a person's future existence and hinders his or her progression toward eternal bliss.

Likewise, reports Buddhist scholar Ian Harris,

> the Buddhist attitude towards animals is essentially instrumental. Its essential function is to aid the practitioner in his search for spiritual perfection, and any good done . . . is merely a happy side-effect. . . .
>
> Concern for the animal kingdom is compatible with Buddhism but does not arise naturally from its central insights into the nature of reality. It can happily be taken along as baggage on the path to perfection, but at some stage it must be abandoned. In actual fact, many of the practices which seem, at one level, to be targeted at the welfare of animals, have as their ultimate aim the spiritual development of the practitioner. The Buddhist ethic in this area is essentially instrumental.[26]

In sum, any respect for animals in Hinduism or Buddhism can be viewed with skepticism as a *side effect* of the doctrines of *ahimsa* and the transmigration of souls. It is not a religious principle mandated by deity to protect animals for their own sake or the overall ecological welfare of nature.

Nature Religions and Deep Ecology

Elements of animism, pantheism, and ancient paganism have recently coalesced in a rapidly growing "new spirituality" movement often referred to by the umbrella term, *nature religions.* The most familiar forms are several varieties of neo-druidism, Wicca (witchcraft), and Gaia. Nature religions often blend various religious ideas and practices drawn from a variety of cultural and political ideologies. Generally, however, all of them are characterized by the belief that the earth is intrinsically sacred and should be revered. Humans, like all living things, are products of evolution and therefore united to all other life forms in some kind of mystical organic whole. For some earth worshippers, this translates into the entire biosphere being a conscious living entity. Thus, people have no special status or rights in nature and no special privileges beyond that of other creatures. Harming nature in any way is a desecrating act.

If all this sounds familiar, it's probably because you watched the 2009 blockbuster movie, *Avatar*. Through the pretentious and misleading medium of Hollywood entertainment, many false and dangerous elements of neo-pagan nature religions were portrayed with engaging and dramatic flair. The movie was clearly designed to juxtapose the eco-friendly, nature loving Na'vi—who lived in worshipful harmony with the oneness of nature—with the single-minded, destructive, eco-insensitive everyman of traditional Western culture.

One might assume that the pro-environment, ecologically conscious philosophy of neo-pagan and other nature religions would grant them greater influence in harnessing destructive environmental practices. It hasn't. As Christian environmentalist Loren Wilkinson pointed out, neo-pagan and other "new spirituality" movements (including Christian) have done little to lessen "the growing engine of economic globalization, with its tendency to ignore the limits of creation in pursuit of the creation of wealth. . . . So despite the appearance of various 'Earth' or 'creation' spiritualities, human behavior has not changed much"[27] in terms of reining in hostile and damaging environmental exploitation.

In other words, in spite of their ecological sensitivity and sometimes aggressive environmental activism, nature religions have failed to foster an environmental ethos that has broad appeal beyond their own (although admittedly growing) inner circle of adherents. Hence, the human race has continued its destructive agenda virtually unabated.

I believe that not only have neo-pagans and other nature religions failed to curtail environmental abuse (just like the other religions we examined in this chapter), but also they have become an *impediment* to formulating real solutions to environmental abuse and harmful exploitation because they inhibit Christian involvement. Here's why.

Many Christians and other conservatives have come to associate neo-paganism with environmentalism. For this reason many shy away from engaging in pro-environmental activities. A pastor recently told me, for example, that he believed the alleged one-world religion described in Revelation 13:11–18 would not be Islam or some other traditional religion, but environmentalism. Although I strongly disagree with this view, it illustrates the widespread assumption among Christians that pagan nature religions are intrinsic to environmentalism.[28]

I recently had a conversation with another Christian that illustrates a similar reason many Christians are reluctant to support environmentalism. This person argued that *all* environmentalists believe that nonhuman life is as valuable as people. A radical faction of environmentalism, referred to as "deep ecology," does consider plants and animals, as well as natural objects (lakes, rivers, mountains, etc.), as possessing intrinsic value equal to humans. Although deep ecologists are philosophically similar to neo-pagans, they embrace a more naturalistic, quasi-scientific rather than spiritual justification for their ecological beliefs.[29]

In response to this challenge, I pointed out that extremists of any ilk do not represent rank-and-file environmentalism. During the past thirty-plus years I have been a member of several non-Christian environmental organizations. I've never met anyone who worshipped nature or believed that animals and natural objects are as valuable as people. The majority love outdoor activities and merely want to enjoy nature, set aside natural habitats, prevent the extinction of wildlife, and manage natural resources in an environmentally sensitive fashion. I'm sure few Christians would object to these goals.

The Human Element

Today, many environmentalists and ecologists recognize that prioritizing human needs is a necessary ingredient in modern conservation. For example, The Nature Conservancy's chief scientist and leader of the organization's 500-plus associated scientists and ecologists, Peter Kareiva, states that the "ultimate goal" of conservation should be "better management of nature for human benefit."[30] He argues that for people to willingly advance conservation efforts, fulfilling human needs must become more relevant in terms of overall ecological and environmental strategies:

> The modern conservation movement has been naïve in its strategies of defending nature *against* . . . human goals.
>
> We must have a vision of the future in which the needs of people and nature are balanced. . . .
>
> The key is to take each of the major needs of people—water, food, livelihoods, security and health—and find the future that meets these needs and protects nature.[31]

CEO and president of The Nature Conservancy, Mark Tercek, agrees: "People are inextricable part of virtually every ecosystem on the planet, . . . and people depend on nature for their survival. The better we are at ensuring that people get [nature's] benefits, the better we'll be at doing conservation."[32]

The ecological philosophy of nature religions and deep ecologists—that nature must be preserved for its "intrinsic worth" without considering human priorities—is not a viable option for reaching long-term conservation goals. People are more likely to endorse and participate in conservation activities if protecting nature and the environment is inclusive of human requirements. I believe this is how the majority of environmentalists feel—and it is in perfect harmony with biblical environmentalism.

The fact is *no one* actually lives according to the belief that nonhumans, natural objects, and people are equal in value. Virtually every day people confront circumstances in which the welfare of nature butts up against the welfare of people. It may be as simple as how to deal with gophers destroying the grass in your yard or as serious as whether to let people go hungry just to avoid developing vital cropland. Such conflicts illustrate a hierarchy in terms of the value of competing life forms. If an issue puts the health and welfare of people in jeopardy, the inevitable decision must always support human life over animal life and natural objects. That's just the way it is—and should be. We can be certain that neo-pagans and deep ecologists will relinquish their closely held beliefs if it means *their* children will go hungry or cannot benefit from lifesaving drugs—even if procuring them negatively affects nature.

❖ ❖

It should be obvious by now that any concern for nonhuman life and natural objects present in animistic tribal cultures, Eastern religions, and neo-paganism is not a religiously based ethical principle designed to protect nature and its creatures for their own sake. In the case of tribal religions, it's a by-product of appeasing a hostile spirit world that supposedly permeates nature. Eastern religion's so-called compassion for nature is equally human-centered. If *ahimsa* and the law of karma instruct followers to avoid harming other animals, the purpose is to aid people in achieving eternal bliss—not to protect wildlife for wildlife's sake. The Buddhist teaching that practitioners should deny self and control consumption is not designed to conserve natural resources; it's to aid one in achieving Nirvana by removing cravings. In neo-paganism, deifying nature has had little impact curtailing environmental abuse, nor does it appeal to rank-and-file environmentalists. In all three religions, there is no accountability to a transcendent divine Authority and thus no objective foundation on which to establish environmental ethics.

Biblical Christianity, on the other hand, reveals that the natural world is the creation of a loving Supreme Being who is concerned about its welfare. Only biblical Christianity recognizes that mankind possesses distinct stewardship responsibilities over creation according to a divine plan. Only biblical Christianity provides the objective moral principles needed to establish environmental ethics and to provide guidance for environmental stewardship. Demonstrating this will be the subject of parts two and three of this book.

Before we explore this, however, one more challenge needs to be addressed—and this one often arises from the ranks of Christendom itself. Many people today are convinced that the earth is relatively healthy, and that most alleged environmental problems are highly exaggerated, if not outright fraudulent. Is this true? Or are serious environmental problems threatening nature and, consequently, the human race? This question will be addressed in the next chapter.

CHAPTER FOUR

THE ENVIRONMENTAL CRISIS: FACT OR FICTION?

A legend perpetrated by childhood cartoons claims the ostrich will stick its head in the sand when frightened. Supposedly, the bird believes an enemy can't see it if it can't see the enemy.[1] Although merely a legend, I sometimes wonder if there is such thing as an *ostrich syndrome*. I've known a few radical anti-environmentalists who appear to suffer from it. Recently, I've had several conversations with a Christian friend over various environmental issues that illustrate this. His response is always predictable: disdain. He is so programmed by the anti-environmental party line that virtually any alleged environmental problem is merely a fabrication of the liberal imagination. To him environmentalists are far-left, tree-hugging radicals who oppose any economic development that may even slightly damage nature or threaten wildlife. And that's all there is to it.

It is true that there *are* overzealous environmental advocates and laws that defy common sense; in fact, some are patently absurd. A case in point was reported in a San Diego newspaper. Apparently, the city of Encinitas, north of San Diego, wanted to obtain a permit to transport sand from a construction project to one of the city's narrow beaches, not an unreasonable request. But to begin, the project required approval from the U.S. Environmental Protection Agency, U.S. Army Corps of Engineers, U.S. Fish and Wildlife Service, California State Lands Commission, California Coastal Commission, two state departments, and the San Diego Association of Governments—a total of eight separate agencies![2] It's no wonder practical-minded people sometimes get frustrated with governmental bureaucracies and vent their anger against environmentalists.

Be this as it may, my friend's attitude was only slightly less ridiculous. The mind-set that all environmentalists are "wackos" not only hinders real progress in identifying and formulating strategies to combat potentially serious environmental problems, but it gives Christianity an ecological black eye. Which brings us to the topic of this chapter.

I stated in the introduction that *Should Christians Be Environmentalists?* is not written to detail or appraise environmental issues. Anyone with Internet access can get an overdose of information on environmental problems. Having said this, however, it will be helpful to dedicate a chapter to highlighting the kinds of environmental problems confronting the earth that are related to human activities. This will demonstrate that the modern environmental crisis is a real and present danger.

Climate Change

Let's start with the most controversial issue. It appears to be fairly certain that climate change (global warming) is occurring. Few scientists today would disagree, even among conservatives. The controversy over climate change is not whether the earth is warming; the debate is whether it's human caused (at least in part) or if the earth is experiencing a normal warming cycle like those that have occurred in the past. For example, former NASA scientist Roy Spencer—whom conservative talk radio host Rush Limbaugh refers to as "the official climatologist" of his talk show—agrees that global warming is happening but suggests that other factors besides human activities are causing it. He believes that it may be resulting from "ocean-based weather patterns."[3]

There have been hundreds (thousands?) of books, editorials, op-ed pieces, research papers, and magazine, newspaper, Internet and journal articles written on this subject—as well as TV documentaries and news features. Many of them put forward contradicting reports and studies. The fact is, no one knows for certain if, or how much, climate change is due to human activities. However, although there is evidence supporting both sides of the debate, the majority of climate scientists do believe that human activities are contributing to global warming. According to a 2009 poll conducted by the University of Illinois Chicago, 97 percent of climate scientists believe human activities are "a significant factor" in climate change.[4] (The poll would obviously include those who are Christians.)

Still, not everyone agrees with these figures. E. Calvin Beisner, national spokesman for the Cornwall Alliance for the Stewardship of Creation, insists "the wheels are coming off the consensus bandwagon. Study after study reduces the magnitude of estimated human contribution to global warming." He reports that "a new study . . . covering the period of 2004 through early 2007 found that the proportion of scientific papers endorsing the 'consensus' [that climate change is largely a result of human activities] had fallen. . . ."[5] And so the debate continues.

What can be said with a great deal of scientific support is that as greenhouse gases have increased in the atmosphere, the earth has been warming. The question remains, however, whether there is a direct correlation between the two. My goal in this chapter is not to express an opinion but to introduce some of the evidence supporting both sides of the debate.

At the outset it can be stated that some of the alleged evidence for human-caused global warming is unashamedly marred by alarmist hype, misinformation, and questionable assumptions leading to faulty inferences.[6] This doesn't win the argument for opponents of global warming, but it does fuel their claim that global warming is more science fiction than scientific.

Having said this, the fact remains that there is compelling scientific evidence that the earth is warming. Some of this evidence is empirical and observable. Scientists have documented, for example, that glaciers and ice sheets in the polar regions have receded at alarming rates. During the last decades, the Greenland Ice Sheet (ice cap) and Antarctica have been losing ice volume due to melting ice and calving icebergs. The same is occurring in the United States.

I visited Montana's Glacier National Park for the first time in 2005. Fewer than thirty glaciers remain in the park, down from 150 a century ago. The glaciers that remain are mere remnants of their former size; some had lost 10 percent of their mass in just the previous seven years. The *only* explanation for melting glaciers and ice sheets is warming temperatures, whether caused by natural climatic changes, some other natural phenomena, or by an increase in greenhouse gases likely due to human activities.[7] Or both.

The United States Global Change Research Project (USGCRP) is one of the largest and most comprehensive scientific studies ever made on global climate change. It began as a presidential initiative in 1989 and was mandated by Congress in the Global Change Research Act of 1990. Its stated purpose was "a comprehensive and integrated United States research program which will assist the Nation and the world to understand, assess, predict, and respond to human-induced *and* natural processes of global change." Thirteen federal departments and agencies participated in the study between 1989 and 2002, including the National Science Foundation, Smithsonian Institution, and the Environmental Protection Agency. The report's conclusions are based on hundreds of studies and measurements collected from thousands of weather stations, ships, and buoys around the world, and from satellites. The data has been independently compiled, analyzed, and processed by numerous research groups. The full report is available online.[8]

Among other things, the report states that temperatures recorded over the last several decades reveal that average global surface temperatures have "increased substantially since 1970" and that all climate models[9] forecast that human-caused emissions of heat-trapping gases will cause further warming in the future. Furthermore:

> The increase in the carbon dioxide concentration has been the principal factor causing warming over the past 50 years. Its concentration has been building up in the Earth's atmosphere since the beginning of the industrial era in the mid-1700s,

primarily due to burning of fossil fuels (coal, oil, and natural gas) and the clearing of forests. . . . The concentration of carbon dioxide in the atmosphere has increased by roughly 35 percent since the start of the industrial revolution.[10]

Another scientific body that evaluates whether or not climate change is related to human activity is the Intergovernmental Panel on Climate Change (IPCC), which was established in 1988 by the World Meteorological Organization (WMO) and the United Nations Environmental Programme (UNEP). The IPCC does not carry out its own research but publishes special reports on the topic. Its conclusions emphatically blame climate change on greenhouse gases: "Warming of the climate system is unequivocal, as is now evident from observations of increases in global average air and ocean temperatures, widespread melting of snow and ice and raising global average sea level."[11] "Most of the observed increase in global average temperatures since the mid-20th century is *very likely* due to the observed increase in anthropogenic [human caused] GHG [greenhouse gas] concentrations."[12]

In spite of the blunt claims of the IPCC reports, the question these and other studies raise is not whether greenhouse gases have increased substantially in the earth's atmosphere over previous decades—it's well documented they have—but whether this has actually contributed to climate change. The definitive answer is yet to be established, although mounting evidence suggests that it is. Still, there is some room for doubt. The USGCRP report points out that "climate changes that have occurred over the last century are not solely caused by human and natural factors."[13] A report from the Environmental Protection Agency states that it cannot be proven "that rising levels of greenhouse gases in the atmosphere are contributing to climate change."[14]

Many scientists insist that *natural* factors are the real cause of climate change. Fluctuations in earth's climate can result from minor changes in the earth's orbit or tilt, affecting the amount of sunlight reaching the planet. Changes in the sun's energy output could induce climate change.

Volcanic eruptions, which can spew huge amounts of carbon dioxide into the atmosphere, can create an increased greenhouse effect, triggering climate changes for short periods of time (two or three years). However, the amount of carbon dioxide produced by volcanoes is "miniscule compared to the human contribution."[15]

So there are clearly two sides to the debate. A variety of empirical evidences indicate the earth is presently warming, and this is likely due to human activities.[16] The opposing view flatly disputes this claim, and points out that climate change is nothing new in the earth's history and a variety of causes could account for it. Human activities may have little to do with it.[17]

Unfortunately, disputes over climate change can be as much about ideology as science. Roy Spencer—Limbaugh's favored climatologist—correctly observes that one of the motivations behind the global warming debate (on both sides of the issue) is religious conviction. Spencer himself "acknowledges that his own evangelical beliefs have predisposed him to follow an opposite path" from many scientists in terms of the resiliency of nature.[18]

It's too bad that more climatologists are not as open and willing to acknowledge their own biases. It would go a long way in focusing the debate on purely scientific data, where it belongs. Be this as it may, as the global warming debate continues, and as more data is collected, it's important for both sides to remember that the jury is still out on the ultimate *cause* of climate change. It is prudent that policy makers not be hasty and dismiss evidence from either side of the debate without thorough examination and further research.

Pollution

Designate a place outside the camp where you can go to relieve yourself. As part of your equipment have something to dig with, and when you relieve yourself, dig a hole and cover up your excrement. (Deut. 23:12–13)

When I read this passage in Deuteronomy, it reminds me of my days with the Sierra Club. In 1981 my wife and I and several friends took a Club course on basic mountaineering. One of their requirements was that on every hike or backpack participants had to carry the "10 Essentials": map and compass, first aid kit, flashlight, and so on. There was also an unofficial "11th essential": toilet paper and a small hand trowel to bury your waste. It's noteworthy that this requirement to curb pollution was mandated by God thousands of years before the Sierra Club or modern environmental laws.

The existence of air and water pollution is one environmental problem with which few people would argue. Anyone living in urban and suburban areas—which comprise about 70 percent of the U.S. population—can testify to air pollution. All you have to do is go outside on a smoggy day. Likewise, most people know that many of America's lakes and rivers have various degrees of pollution. In the 1960s and 1970s, I had no qualms drinking water directly from mountain lakes and streams. Not so today. Even in wilderness areas, many backpackers carry water-filtering devices and refuse to drink water directly from lakes and streams.

The major sources of air pollution are industrial and automobile emissions. In the case of water pollution, it's effluents (liquid industrial waste and sewage) discharged into water and soil. The good news is that the United States is far ahead of many nations in terms of regulating air and water pollution. The Clean Air Act (1963, amended in 1977 and 1990) and the Clean Water Act (i.e., the Federal Water Pollution Control Act of 1972, amended in 1977) have made significant progress in ensuring the quality of America's air and water. Even so, the United States remains one of the world's leaders in air pollution emissions.

Air and water pollution is not confined to international borders, and it's poorly regulated in many countries. Vast areas of the earth are affected—especially China, Russia, Mexico, and Japan. According to a *New York Times* article, a World Bank study reported that 750,000 people in China die every year as a result of air and water pollution.[19]

Not surprisingly, air and water pollution also affects nonhuman life.

When sulfur dioxide and nitrogen oxides from fossil fuel combustion react in the atmosphere with water, oxygen, and other chemicals, it creates sulfuric acid and nitric acid—what's referred to as "acid rain." This solution has polluted entire lakes in Europe and the United States, especially in Eastern states, killing fish and aquatic plant life and causing soils to become so toxic that plants cannot grow. Smog can also reduce the amount of sunlight available for plants, reducing photosynthesis and thereby affecting other organisms in the food chain. Even the vast oceans, which comprise three-quarters of the earth's surface, are being affected by pollution. Research sponsored by the National Science Foundation, the National Oceanic and Atmospheric Administration, and the U.S. Geological Survey presented "indisputable" evidence that air pollution is "rapidly raising the acidity of the world's oceans, threatening widespread destruction of the tiny shell-building organisms that form the base of the entire marine food web and create coral reefs."[20]

Habitat Loss

As with air and water pollution, most people are familiar with habitat loss. Since World War II, the population of the United States has about doubled, and the conversion of open space into suburban and industrial development has escalated proportionately. According to the U.S. Department of Agriculture, "between 1992–1997, [America] lost 11.2 million acres worth of farmland and other open spaces to sprawl." This amounts to 2.2 million acres annually.[21]

Suburban and commercial development, however, is just the tip of the iceberg when it comes to habitat loss on a global scale. The most widespread and destructive cause of habitat loss is deforestation. By 1990, worldwide deforestation had increased to "some 100,000 square kilometers of primary forest—an area the size of Iceland" every year.[22] As a result, about half of the world's forests have been destroyed, primarily to produce fuel, manufacture lumber, and clear land for farming. To this day, another 13 million hectares of forest are destroyed annually.[23]

The United States ranks seventh in the world as having the largest annual loss of old growth forest (Cambodia had the highest deforestation rate).[24] Centuries ago, "almost half of the United States, three-quarters of Canada, almost all of Europe . . . and much of the rest of the world were forested."[25] Since the 1600s, 90 percent of America's original forests in the lower forty-eight states have been destroyed, especially in the Eastern United States. In the Western states, many forests continue to be threatened, with about 80 percent of the old growth forests remaining in the Pacific Northwest slated for logging.[26] Altogether, America is losing forestland at the rate of 900,000 acres per year, with 60,000 of those acres "ancient forests."[27]

Deforestation (along with desertification) is an ancient problem, and one of the major contributors to worldwide environmental change—including the loss of unknown numbers of plant and animal species. Historically, most deforestation occurred in Europe, North America, North Africa, and the Middle East. In the twentieth century, however, it began to increase dramatically in developing nations, especially in Africa and South America. In particular, over the last few decades, massive deforestation has taken place in the tropics, which is home to an estimated 40 to 75 percent of the world's remaining plant and animal species. According to satellite surveys of the Amazon rain forest in Brazil, 437 square miles of forest were cut down or burned in the single month of April 2008.[28] Should the current rate continue, "the world's rain forests will vanish within 100 years—causing unknown effects on global climate and eliminating the majority of plant and animal species on the planet."[29]

Deforestation not only directly affects indigenous plants and animals, but potentially the entire human race. Local deforestation can create microclimate changes, resulting in less regional rainfall. Worldwide, deforestation can potentially alter climates across the globe by raising the level of greenhouse gases in the atmosphere: "Burning of forests releases about two billion metric tons of carbon dioxide into the atmosphere each year, or about 22 percent of anthropogenic [human caused] emission of carbon."[30] This results when forests are cleared with fire, releasing into the atmosphere carbon stored in the wood.

On the flip side, the value of rainforests is incalculable. Through photosynthesis, 28 percent of the world's oxygen originates from rainforests.[31] During this process, tropical forests sequester carbon from the atmosphere, helping to control the buildup of greenhouse gases. Unfortunately, at today's emission rates, plant life cannot absorb and store the amount of carbon currently being released through industry, deforestation, and automobile emissions. Thus, the continual rise of greenhouse gases in the atmosphere. The vast tropical green world also supplies medicines and balms used in curing many sicknesses and diseases. The extinction of plant species in the tropics could curtail future discoveries of new lifesaving drugs.

Extinction

Plant and animal extinction is a natural part of nature. Thousands of animals that once roamed the earth no longer exist. Although on occasion mass extinctions have occurred, generally, extinction rates have been a relatively slow process. On a geological time scale,[32] according to award-winning author and environmental correspondent Julia Whitty, "background" (natural) extinction rates are estimated to have been "about one species per million per year."[33] At least that was the rate until the twentieth century. The extinction rate today may be one hundred times the background rate. According to mathematical computer models—which are not necessarily always accurate—some biologists estimate that the extinction rate today could be as high as a thousand times the background rate, with a minimum of about three species becoming extinct *every day!*[34] Explained Whitty: "In the 21st century the rate [of extinction] is nothing short of explosive. . . . More than 16,000 species of the world's mammals, birds, plants and other organisms are at present officially regarded as threatened with extinction to one degree or another, according to Red List." (The World Conservation Union's Red List is a database tracking the global status of earth's 1.5 million scientifically named animal species.[35] There may be ten million or more plant and animal species yet to be discovered.) Whitty continued:

When we hear of extinction, most of us think of the plight of the rhino, tiger, panda or blue whale. But these sad sagas are only small pieces of the extinction puzzle. The overall numbers are terrifying. Of the 40,168 species that the 10,000 scientists in the World Conservation Union have assessed, one in four mammals, one in eight birds, one in three amphibians, one in three conifers and other gymnosperms are at risk of extinction. The peril faced by other classes of organisms is less thoroughly analyzed, but fully 40 percent of the examined species of planet earth are in danger, including perhaps 51 percent of reptiles, 52 percent of insects, and 73 percent of flowering plants.[36]

There is a point of no return with regard to animal populations. If the numbers of a particular species of plant or animal decrease below a certain point or become spread too far apart, they may become genetically weakened and vulnerable to localized natural disasters. Even minor events such as "a passing thunderstorm; an unexpected freeze; drought. At fewer than fifty members, populations experience increasing random fluctuations until a kind of fatal arrhythmia takes hold. Eventually, an entire genetic legacy . . . is removed from the future."[37]

What is causing today's worldwide and greatly accelerated mass extinction of plants and animals? There are a number of factors, but virtually all are related to human activities. Since the highest concentration of plant and animal species is found in the tropics, deforestation has been a major factor in plant and animal extinction. This is one reason that the preservation of the world's remaining old growth forests is a top priority of conservationists.

According to Whitty, the primary causes of extinction today are "habitat degradation, overexploitation, agricultural monocultures, human-borne invasive species, [and] human-induced climate-change."[38] In the case of many species of animals, illegal poaching and unrestricted hunting are also major threats to their survival. The classic example in the United States is the passenger pigeon.

The last passenger pigeon (Martha) died September 1, 1914, in the Cincinnati Zoo. (I wonder what God thought about that!) During the nineteenth century, passenger pigeons were probably the most numerous birds on the planet; an estimated three to five *billion* lived in North America before the arrival of Europeans. Migratory flocks a mile wide and up to 300 long had been reported, some so dense they darkened the sky for hours and even days as they flew overhead. Sadly, by the early nineteenth century, passenger pigeon populations began to decline, with catastrophic declines between 1870 and 1890. Commercial hunters killed most of the birds to provide inexpensive food and, sometimes, as live targets for trap shooting and for agricultural fertilizers.[39]

Perhaps the most frightening extinction scenario in recent times is described in an article published in the journal *Science.* Biologists believe the entire class of Amphibia (amphibians) may be threatened with extinction—and up to 122 species have already become extinct since 1980.[40] According to researchers from numerous fields, over the past two decades the earth's amphibians (frogs, salamanders, newts, and toads) have experienced a rapid, global die-off—some species vanishing in as little as six months. The suspected cause is a rapidly spreading fungal disease (*Batrachochytrium dendrobatidis*), along with pollution, pesticides, habitat loss, climate change, commercial over exploitation, ultraviolet radiation, and invasive species.[41]

Amphibians are a food source for fish, birds, snakes, and many other animals. Their extinction from the food chain could seriously threaten the continued existence of wildlife that depend on them for food. But this isn't the worst-case scenario. Scientists point out that a massive die-off of amphibians could be a harbinger of an unprecedented ecological crisis. Amphibians are more susceptible to changes in the environment than most animals. In nature, amphibians have been likened to canaries in a coal mine. Before modern sensors, canaries were used to alert miners if the air in a mine became toxic; if the canaries died, the air was becoming poisonous. Amphibian skin absorbs both water and oxygen. Thus, their survival depends on a healthy, pollution-free environment. If the entire class of Amphibia becomes extinct, it could indicate that the earth's eco-systems have become so deteriorated that all life on earth is in danger.

❖   ❖

This has been a brief survey of the four varieties of environmental problems caused by and confronting the human race (and nature). Although limited in scope, it is sufficient to answer three important questions relevant to mankind's negative impact on creation. First, is the environmental crisis real ("fact or fiction") and growing in severity? Yes, it is. Second, is mankind *corporately* responsible for this degradation? Again, the answer is yes. Third, will humanity be held accountable for exploiting and despoiling nature? Yes we will, and in two ways. First, on an ecological level, Homo sapiens are members of the earth's biosphere. We depend upon a healthy environment to survive, just as all the other inhabitants of earth do. When nature suffers, humanity suffers. Climate change, pollution, habitat loss, and extinction can have long-range and devastating consequences for the entire human race.

There is a second reason people will be held accountable for exploiting and despoiling nature, and we'll examine this in detail in the following chapters. Briefly stated, God instructed the human race to be His stewards, His caretakers, over creation. Failure to obey this charge has not only resulted in today's environmental crisis, but it also has moral and theological ramifications. This brings us to part 2 of our study.

PART TWO

A BIBLE-BASED
THEOLOGY OF NATURE

CHAPTER FIVE

CREATION

God's Love for, Providence over, and Provision for Nature

> *You alone are the LORD. You made the heavens, even the*
> *highest heavens, and all their starry host, the earth and all*
> *that is on it, the seas and all that is in them. You give life*
> *to everything, and the multitudes of heaven worship you.*
>
> Nehemiah 9:6

The author of Nehemiah (probably Ezra) beautifully and worshipfully put into words a belief that is fundamental to both Christians and Jews—and one that is expressed throughout the Bible. God is the author of life. He is the Creator of all that exists: the star-filled heavens, the earth, and life on land and in the seas. No other creation story in any religion has such a precise and clearly defined account of origins as the Bible. The doctrine of creation is the foundation of biblical environmental ethics and stewardship.

Professors Denise and John Carmody have correctly observed that "Ecology has come rather late to most Christian consciousness, but an ecologically sensitive Christian outlook could be as near as a rereading of the Christian doctrine of creation."[1] The foundation of such a doctrine is stated in the first verse of the first chapter in the Bible: "In the beginning God created the heavens and the earth" (Gen. 1:1). The significance of this short introductory statement cannot be overemphasized. Without a personal God who willfully chose to create, there could be no absolute theological or moral basis for environmental ethics and stewardship.

Moreover, a God who purposely created nature would logically be concerned for its welfare and would put measures into place to care for it. As we saw in chapter 3, the abstract, impersonal, non-creating god of Eastern religions has neither the ability nor a reason to be concerned with environmental matters.

Foundational Doctrines

Besides the *fact* of creation, five interrelated sub-doctrines within the biblical doctrine of creation are foundational to developing a theology of nature, which will culminate in a Bible-based environmental doctrine.[2]

God Transcends Creation

The Bible teaches that God is the creator of all that exists—both animate and inanimate—here on earth as well as throughout the entire cosmos (the "heavens"). In order to be such a Creator, God must *transcend* nature; that is, He is distinct and apart from creation by virtue of being its Creator. A transcendent God would also exist *prior* to what He created. Both these characteristics rule out pantheism because creation (and thus nature) cannot be a manifestation of God's "essence." Moreover, if God transcends creation and exists apart from it, nature cannot be divine. God's transcendence precludes and forbids pagan nature religions that worship creation rather than the Creator (Rom. 1:21–25).

God Is Immanent Throughout His Creation

God not only transcends nature, He is also *immanent* throughout it. The Spirit of God is omnipresent, throughout the entire created cosmos, and nature is full of manifestations that express His presence. The psalmist enthusiastically declared, "The heavens declare the glory of God; the skies proclaim the work of his hands" (Ps. 19:1). The apostle Paul reminds us that God's "eternal power and divine nature" are clearly seen through creation (Rom. 1:20).

Now, Christians must be careful here. There is a fundamental difference between the biblical doctrine of God's immanence *to* nature and pantheism's philosophy that God's all-encompassing essence *includes* nature. Pantheists look at a tree or mountain and believe that they are *part of* God's substance. Christians, on the other hand, acknowledge that God is totally aware of every particle and process inclusive of the tree or mountain, but the tree or mountain is not part of God. Jesus said that not one sparrow falls to the ground but that the Father knows it. God even numbers the very hairs on our head (Matt. 10:29–30). But nowhere in Scripture is nature identified as God in substance or essence. God's transcendence apart from creation makes His immanence vastly different from pantheism. We can observe God's glory and power in nature because He created it, but we cannot see God Himself. Nature is not God and God is not nature.

Similarly, Christians must not confuse God's immanence (presence) throughout nature with the animist's belief that spirits indwell objects in nature, such as animals, rivers, or sacred mountains. The Bible teaches that nature reveals God's presence, but He does not lurk about or dwell within the objects He created. Again, nature is not divine. God's immanence allows people to experience His glory and power in nature without fear of evil spirits or engaging in idolatry. C. S. Lewis remarked on this: "It is surely just because the natural objects are no longer taken to be themselves divine that they can now be magnificent symbols of Divinity. . . . By emptying Nature of divinity—or, let us say, of divinities—you may fill her with Deity, for she is now the bearer of messages."[3] The book of Job beautifully expresses God's immanence to His creation through a series of rhetorical questions that He asked Job. Chapters 38 and 39 are particularly relevant. It is noteworthy that although spoken to Job, these passages describe natural phenomena in which the presence of people is absent. For example, in Job 38:25–26 God gives rain "to water a land where no man lives, a desert with no one in it." Similarly in 39:6 He gives the wild donkey "the wasteland as his home, the salt flats as his habitat." God asked Job, "Where does light come from, and where does darkness go?" (38:19 NASB); "Have you entered the storehouses of the snow or seen the storehouses of the hail?" (38:22); "Do you know when the mountain goats give birth? Do you watch when the doe bears her fawn?" (39:1). The self-evident answers, of course, are that only God observes these events and is present when they occur. It is God's immanence throughout nature that allows Him to witness all of the events related in Job 38 and 39.

God Maintains Nature

The third significant sub-doctrine of creation is that God actively maintains (upholds and sustains) nature. Colossians 1:17 states that God, through Jesus Christ, "is before all things, and in him all things hold together." The author of Hebrews wrote, "The Son is the radiance of God's glory and the exact representation of his being, sustaining all things by his powerful word" (1:3). The psalmist wrote that God

> covers the sky with clouds;
> he supplies the earth with rain
> and makes grass grow on the hills.
> He provides food for the cattle
> and for the young ravens when they call.
> (147:8–9; see also Ps. 148)

Psalm 104 further reveals God's active involvement throughout nature: God "makes springs pour water into the ravines" (v. 10), and "waters the mountains" (v. 13), and all animals look to God "to give them their food at the proper time" (v. 27). Environmental ethicist Loren Wilkinson explained, "God's creative acts are here presented [in Psalm 104] not as taking place in some archetypal beginning but as happening continually, *now*."[4]

Every detail of creation, including what we refer to as "natural laws," reflects God's *continuous* activity in nature. The book of Job recounts that God "cuts a channel for the torrents of rain, and a path for the thunderstorm" (38:25). It is God "who appoints the sun to shine by day, who decrees the moon and stars to shine by night, who stirs up the sea so that its waves roar" (Jer. 31:35). God set up the seasons of the year (Gen. 8:22) and appointed the time for harvest (Jer. 5:24). Lightning, hail, snow, clouds, and stormy winds all operate at God's bidding (Ps. 148:8). God sends the rain and makes grass grow on the mountains (Ps. 147:8), causes the snow to melt in spring (Ps. 147:18), and gives flowers their beauty (Matt. 6:29–30). God gives life to animals, establishes their territories, and provides their daily food (Job 38:41; Ps. 104:14–30; Joel 2:22).

Nature is not a self-contained, self-organized system of randomly evolving natural laws. Rather, just like ours, nature's existence depends moment to moment on the attention and vigilance of God's continuous care and sustaining power and love. God is not only the Creator, but He also maintains all natural processes (also see Job 37:6, 10–13; Ps. 147:8, 16–18; Jer. 10:13).

God Made Man in His Own Image

It is rightfully said that God had the human race in mind when He created planet earth (Ps. 115:16).[5] Yet, in terms of purely *physical* creation, human beings are no different than animals. Both people and animals were created on the same day (day six of the creation week); God did not set aside a special day to create the human race. God said to Job, "Look at the behemoth, which I made along with you" (Job 40:15). Likewise, speaking of the physical body, Solomon wrote, "Man's fate is like that of the animals; the same fate awaits them both: As one dies, so dies the other. All have the same breath; man has no advantage over the animal. . . . All go to the same place; all come from dust, and to dust all return" (Eccl. 3:19–20).

Homo sapiens, plants, and animals, are living organisms who depend on a healthy physical environment in order to survive. Indeed, like all creatures, humans must use other life forms for our own survival and prosperity. The human race is a member (ecologically speaking) of the "great chain of life" that exists within the complex, interrelated biosphere of planet earth. God provides for our physical needs no differently than He provides for the needs of other life forms—through our natural environment. Thus, human beings have a "kinship" relationship with other created life because we depend on God, through nature, to provide our food and shelter the same as He does for wild animals (Job 12:10).

This is only half the biblical story. The Bible also reveals that people have an exalted position in creation (Matt. 6:26; 10:31; 12:11–12). We are the "crown" of God's creation, the culmination of the creation week. The psalmist wrote,

> What is man that you are mindful of him,
>   the son of man that you care for him?
> You made him a little lower than the heavenly beings
>   and crowned him with glory and honor.
> You made him ruler over the works of your hands;
> You put everything under his feet.
>
> (Ps. 8:4–6)

In order to understand the relationship that exists between people and the rest of creation, it must be understood that the human race has a dual position in creation. Although Homo sapiens are one of countless millions of created life forms, we are unique and special to God (Ps. 139:13–16). Only people were created in His image (Gen. 1:26–27).

What does it mean to be created in God's image? Since God is spirit (John 4:24), being created in His image is something other than a physical likeness. It must be confined to the immaterial part of our being, our soul and spirit, rather than flesh and bones. Moreover, it must also include God-like attributes found only in people. Non-human creatures were not created in God's image. On the other hand, because people are finite and not divine, whatever these attributes may be, they must be immeasurably less manifest in humans than in God.

The majority of theologians agree that being created in God's image relates to things like self-awareness and the capacity to reason and create rather than to react on mere instinct (2 Peter 2:12; Jude 1:10). God-like qualities also include a moral conscience (Rom. 2:13–15; 1 Peter 1:15), free will (Gen. 2:16–17; Rom. 1:18; Eph. 4:18), and the divinely given ability to love unconditionally (*agape*—1 John 4:7–8, 19). These traits differentiate Homo sapiens from animals—and are representative of God's attributes. So although physically, people are members of nature and similar to other creatures in many ways, we are distinct in that we possess personhood and God-like attributes that are endowed with the divine image.

Why is this important in terms of developing an environmental doctrine? To be created in God's image is to be endowed with responsibilities. This, in turn, sheds light on why God commissioned the human race to be His caretakers over creation (we'll explore this later). As His ordained stewards over the environment and nonhuman life, we are to have the same loving concern for nature that God has for nature: care for it, protect it, maintain it, nurture it, even in a sense "save" it (e.g., from destructive exploitation and abuse). Only people possess the God-like attributes necessary to fulfill this moral responsibility.

God Vaules Nature Independent of (but Never Equal to or Above) People

Throughout the Bible, from Genesis 1 (*all* creation is "very good" [v. 31]) through Revelation ("The time has come for . . . destroying those who destroy the earth" [11:18]; i.e., those in rebellion against God often destroy the earth they worship—see Warren Wiersby's commentary on this passage at the end of chapter 8), Scripture reveals that nature and wildlife are valuable to God *independent* of humanity. Five times *before* God created Adam and Eve, He surveyed the progress of the creation week and pronounced it was "good." At the end of the creation week, He proclaimed that *all* creation was "very good." God did not single out people when proclaiming the goodness of nature. From this passage in the first book of the Bible, it appears that nature has value to God in and of itself; that is, independent of the human race.

Sadly, many Christians fail to recognize this. They believe that nature's welfare and value is always subservient to human needs *as well as* desires. I saw a bumper sticker years ago that illustrated this: "Save Babies not Whales." Obviously, the owner of the car was pro-life. That's a good thing. Unfortunately, although the slogan rightfully elevated human life above animal life, it suggested a faulty either/or dilemma (either human life or whale life) that doesn't exist. Abortion should be prevented—and babies *are* more important than whales—but that has nothing to do with whether or not whales should be protected. Of course they should. Whales are some of the most magnificent animals God created, and some varieties are in grave danger of becoming extinct. But saving whales has nothing to do with saving babies. Both humans and whales should be protected, not because they are equal in God's eyes, but because both have value to God independent of each other.

The Bible teaches, as we saw in Psalm 8, that people are the pinnacle of God's creation. Humans are of greater value than animals (Matt. 12:12; Luke 12:7, 24). Moreover, nature is to provide for human needs (Gen. 1:29; 9:3), and the family of man has a right to use it and the authority to "rule" over it (Gen. 1:28). On the other hand, the Bible does not give people permission to exploit nature or abuse the creatures with which we share the planet. They don't belong to us; they belong to God: "To the LORD your God belong the heavens, even the highest heavens, the earth and everything in it" (Deut. 10:14; see also Ps. 24:1; Job 41:11). What's more, the Bible does *not* teach that God created the earth solely for human consumption and comfort. If that were true, why are there tsunamis, earthquakes, hurricanes, scorpions, poison ivy, fleas, cockroaches, and mosquitos to plague the human race? The fact is Scripture reveals that nature has value to God *independent* of humanity. Indeed, God created far more plants and animals than human beings could possibly need for survival. Why? For His own good pleasure—for His own enjoyment (Ps. 104:31–32).

This is contrary to what many non-Christian environmentalists take for granted that Christians believe. They assume that the Bible bestows on human beings carte blanche to use nature at will, even if it results in destructive environmental exploitation. And nowhere, critics claim, is the Bible more anthropocentric and despotic toward nature than its treatment of animals. Animal rights advocate Peter Singer stated, "The New Testament is completely lacking in any injunction against cruelty to animals, or any recommendations to consider their interests. Jesus himself showed indifference to the fate of nonhumans when he induced two thousand swine to hurl themselves into the sea."[6]

We'll examine Jesus' dealings with nature in chapter 12, where I'll demonstrate that His attitude toward nature was *not* "indifference." For now, it's enough to understand that it would be out of character—and theologically impossible, in light of the triune nature of God—for Jesus to have an apathetic attitude toward nature that God the Father does not possess. Whatever the reason that Jesus accommodated the demons' request to be cast into a herd of pigs, it had nothing to do with His love, care, and concern for nature and animal life. (By the way, it was the demons who drove the pigs into the sea, not Jesus [see Matt. 8:30–32].)

Having said this, it is true that some Christians have exploited wildlife and attempted to justify it by appealing to Scriptures. Professor C. F. D. Moule provided a distressing illustration of this. He recounted an experience of otter researcher Gavin Maxwell, who had lost two otter cubs brought back from Nigeria:

> "A minister of the Church of Scotland, walking along the foreshore with a shotgun, found them at play by the tide's edge and shot them. One was killed outright, the other died of her wounds in the water. The minister," added Maxwell bitterly, "expressed regret, but reminded a journalist: 'The Lord gave man control over the beasts of the field.'"[7]

I would argue that *non-Christians* have mistreated animals and killed them without justification as much, if not more, than Christians. Regardless, such heartless and unnecessary killing of harmless wildlife by a clergyman understandably fuels the fiery passion of anti-Christian environmentalists. The question at hand, however, is not whether Christians have mistreated animals more than non-Christians have, but what does the Bible teach with regard to how people *should* treat animals?

Biblical Evidence

The biblical fact is that God loves, provides for, and has great concern for the welfare of animals, and He expects people to model His attitude. The following survey of Bible passages that address God's provision for animals—both wild and domesticated—clearly demonstrates this.

God created a world designed to support animal life as well as human (Ps. 36:6; Isa. 43:20). Jesus said that it is God who feeds the ravens and other birds (Matt. 6:26; Luke 12:24). Before the first creatures were spoken into existence, God created vegetation to produce "plants bearing seed according to their kinds and trees bearing fruit with seed in it according to their kinds" (Gen. 1:12). Thus, food and shelter were available when animal life began to inhabit the earth (v. 30). After their creation, God charged the sea life, the birds of the air, and land dwelling "livestock, creatures that move along the ground, and wild animals" to multiply and fill the seas and cover the earth (vv. 20–25).

Prior to the worldwide flood, God took great care to save both wild and domesticated animals by placing them in the ark with Noah and his family (Gen. 6:19–7:3). God didn't recreate animal life after the flood—He preserved it. Later, when the floodwaters had receded and the animals were released to repopulate the earth (8:17–18), God made a covenant that included *all* animal life as well as humans. Indeed, the covenant included the entire earth (9:13). It was an unconditional, permanent covenant:

> Then God said to Noah and to his sons with him: "I now establish my covenant with you and with your descendants after you and with every living creature that was with you—the birds, the livestock and all the wild animals, all those that came out of the ark with you—every living creature on earth. I establish my covenant with you: Never again will all life be cut off by the waters of a flood; never again will there be a flood to destroy the earth." (Gen. 9:8–11)

The prophet Hosea spoke of another covenant that would occur in the distant, eschatological future that will also include animals:

> In that day I will make a covenant for them
> with the beasts of the field and the birds of the air
> and the creatures that move along the ground.
> Bow and sword and battle
> I will abolish from the land,
> So that all may lie down in safety. (2:18)

Throughout the Old Testament, animals have more than incidental roles in the affairs of people. Part of King Solomon's wisdom was that "he described plant life, from the cedar of Lebanon to the hyssop that grows out of walls. He also taught about animals and birds, reptiles and fish" (1 Kings 4:33). Job told his accusers that people can learn from fish, birds, and other animals (12:7–8). Sometimes God used animals for specific and unusual purposes. When God instructed Elijah to go into hiding, He used ravens to bring the prophet food (1 Kings 17:1–6). God used a great fish to save Jonah's life (Jonah 1:17) and a small fish to provide the money for Jesus and Peter to pay the temple tax (Matt. 17:24–27). Wild animals even accompanied Jesus during His temptation in the wilderness (Mark 1:13). And, strangest of all, in the account of Balaam and his donkey, it was the donkey—not Balaam— that saw the angel sent to prevent Balaam from doing evil (Num. 22).

God further demonstrated His love and care for animals alongside His love and care for people in the Sabbath year instructions given to the Israelites:

> For six years you are to sow your fields and harvest the crops, but during the seventh year let the land lie unplowed and unused. Then the poor among your people may get food from it, and *the wild animals may eat what they leave.* Do the same with your vineyard and your olive grove. (Exod. 23:10–11, emphasis added; see also Lev. 25:1–7)

Elsewhere Moses stated, "If you come across a bird's nest beside the road, either in a tree or on the ground, and the mother is sitting on the young or on the eggs, do not take the mother with the young. You may take the young, but be sure to let the mother go" (Deut. 22:6–7). Here we see instructions to preserve breeding populations of animals harvested for human consumption. Had this injunction been followed in human cultures throughout history, there would be fewer endangered species today.

God is equally concerned that people treat domesticated animals humanely. This is expressed in Proverbs 12:10, "A righteous man cares for the needs of his animal." Similarly, Moses wrote, "Six days do your work, but on the seventh day do not work, so that your ox and your donkey may rest" (Exod. 23:12). Elsewhere Moses wrote, "If you see your brother's donkey or his ox fallen on the road, do not ignore it. Help him get it to its feet" (Deut. 22:4); "Do not muzzle an ox while it is treading out the grain" (i.e., allow it to eat some of the grain; 25:4). God's command to protect domestic animals also includes an *enemy's* livestock (Exod. 23:4–5). Even the Ten Commandments have a provision to care for domesticated animals: "Six days you shall labor and do all your work, but the seventh day is a Sabbath to the LORD your God. On it you shall not do any work, neither you, nor your son or daughter, nor your manservant or maidservant, *nor your animals*" (Exod. 20:9–10, emphasis added). God requires humane treatment for wild *and* domesticated animals.

A fascinating—but less familiar—example of God's concern for domesticated animals is found in Jonah. After the prophet warned the Ninevites that they would be destroyed in forty days unless they repented, the King of Nineveh decreed that not only the people but the domestic animals fast and be covered with sackcloth (Jonah 3:7–8). Later, after the Ninevites repented, God conversed with Jonah (who was still angry because the hated Assyrians were spared) and revealed His compassion not only for the people but for the animals: "Should I not have compassion on Nineveh, the great city in which there are more than 120,000 persons who do not know the difference between their right and left hand, as well as many animals?" (4:11 NASB).

❖ ❖

Why does God express such heartfelt and earnest concern for non-human life? Because God values nature and the animals He created, and He derives immense joy from them: "For every animal of the forest is mine, and the cattle on a thousand hills. I know every bird in the mountains, and the creatures of the field are mine" (Ps. 50:10–11). In response to God's love and provision, through beautiful poetic language, creation worships the Creator with expressions of joy and praises (Ps. 148; see also Pss. 65:12–13; 96:11–12; 98:4–8; Isa. 43:20). Nature praises God and so, as one author put it, "We have to reject the notion that wild nature is only valuable if it is useful to humans. If wild nature praises God, that alone justifies its existence."[8]

Nowhere does the Bible communicate God's love and joy for nature more beautifully, passionately, and poetically than Psalm 104. It recounts how God carefully prepared nature to support plant and animal life. It speaks of forest animals and sea life, of wild donkeys and wild goats, of birds, cattle, rock badgers, and lions. Psalm 104 reveals that all of these creatures depend on God for food and shelter—indeed, for the very breath of life:

> You make the springs pour water into ravines,
> so streams gush down from the mountains.
> They provide water for all the animals,
> and the wild donkeys quench their thirst.
> The birds nest besides the streams
> and sing among the branches of the trees. . . .
> The trees of the LORD are well cared for. . . .
> There the birds make their nests,
> and the storks make their homes in the firs.
> High in the mountain are pastures for the wild goats,
> and the rocks form a refuge for rock badgers. . . .
> You send the darkness, and it becomes night,
> when all the forest animals prowl about.

> Then the young lions roar for their food,
>> but they are dependent on God.
> At dawn they slink back
>> into their dens to rest. . . .
> O Lord, what a variety of things you have made!
>> In wisdom you have made them all.
>> The earth is full of your creatures.
> Here is the ocean, vast and wide,
>> teeming with life of every kind,
>> both great and small. . . .
> Every one of these depends on you
>> to give them their food as they need it.
> When you supply it, they gather it.
>> You open your hand to feed them, and
>> they are satisfied.
> But if you turn away from them, they panic.
>> When you take away their breath, they die
>> and turn again to dust.
> When you send your Spirit, new life is born
>> to replenish all the living of the earth.
>
> (vv. 10–30 NLT)

Does this sound like a God who created nature solely for human consumption and who is "indifferent" to how people treat animals, as Singer and other critics claim? Hardly! Many passages throughout the Bible, especially in Job and the Psalms, portray an entirely different biblical picture of God and nature than what critics allege. The earth belongs to God, not people; He created it. God cares for nature apart from (but not above) His love and care for people. As the psalmist said,

> Your love, O Lord, reaches to the heavens,
>> your faithfulness to the skies.

Your righteousness is like the mighty mountains,
   your justice like the great deep.
O LORD, you preserve both man and beast. (36:5–6)

This fact alone is sufficient reason for the human race to take a caretaker's role over the natural world. As theologian William Dyrness remarked, "Here lies a great justification for the preservation of wilderness areas that exist for no other purpose than to exhibit the greatness of God by preserving his creative work."[9]

But something happened that tarnished the perfection and goodness of God's creation. Due to human sin, nature became marred and corrupted. This tragic story and its consequences are the subject of the next chapter.

CHAPTER SIX

THE FALL

*The Human Race Opens the Door to
Environmental Exploitation and Abuse*

S ecular humanists and New Age practitioners believe that the human race is ascending to ever greater heights of goodness and value. Secular humanists declare that with increased scientific knowledge and technology, the world can reach a state of virtual heaven on earth: no more disease, hunger, poverty, war—perhaps not even death. Similarly, New Agers assert that with greater spiritual insight, the divine potential within humanity will manifest itself and usher in a new age of global prosperity, peace, and world order.

A little reflection and common sense reveals that both views are nonsense.

If Homo sapiens are the result of evolutionary forces—and both of these philosophies are evolutionary in their essential assumptions—why, with the passing of the millennia, has the human race failed to radically improve in the area of ethical behavior? Why has our ability to get along as "social animals" failed to evolve? The fact is people are just as greedy, covetous, selfish, cruel, and warlike today as they have been throughout human history. Indeed, if history were the only criterion, it could be argued that Homo sapiens are *devolving!*

Look at the twentieth century. It was the most bloodthirsty century in human history. Eighty-six million people died fighting wars between 1900 and 1989. An additional 120 million people were killed by government-sponsored genocide and mass murder—80 million of these in two *atheistic* countries: China and the former Soviet Union.[1]

These tragic statistics reveal that something is fundamentally wrong with the human race. It is not evolving to greater goodness, nor do people exhibit the slightest trace of divine potential. On the contrary, the family of man possesses what theologians refer to as a "sin nature," an inherent proclivity to rebel against God and to engage in immoral behavior (Gen. 8:21; Mark 7:20–23; Rom. 7:18–19; Eph. 2:1–3).

In terms of the issue at hand (developing a Bible-based theology of nature), this predisposition to sin also reveals itself in humanity's worldwide inclination to exploit nature for purely selfish and greedy purposes. This is the underlying reason that the human race, in every period of history, in every culture, and under the banner of every religious belief, has exploited its physical environments and exterminated many of the creatures with which we share the earth. I use the phrase *intrinsic exploitive behavior* to describe this conduct.

Does this mean that exploiting nature is sin? It may be a stretch to some theologians to say that people can sin *against* nature—at least directly. However, God decreed the human race to be His stewards—His caretakers—over creation (see chapter 8). People have a moral obligation to manage nature according to this God-ordained directive. Refusing to do this is an act of disobedience to God. Any rebellion against God is sin (1 John 3:4). So, at least indirectly, exploiting nature may be considered sin in the sense that we are morally accountable to God for our decisions and behavior with regard to the well-being of nature.

We'll explore this moral responsibility further in chapter 11. For now, my focus is to explain how this intrinsic exploitive behavior came to be and how it affects mankind's relationship with nature. This is the second step to developing an environmental doctrine. It begins with what Christians refer to as *the fall*.

What Ever Happened to the Human Race?

The origin of all sin, whether against God, people, *or nature*, is rooted in what Christian theologians refer to as "the fall" or "the fall of mankind." In order to understand the reason that enmity exists between people and nature—and thus the source of mankind's intrinsic exploitive behavior—this watershed biblical doctrine must be understood.

On day six of the creation week, after He had created Adam and Eve in His own image (Gen. 1:27), God looked at all He had made and pronounced it "very good" (1:31). The natural environment in which God placed the first couple was (literally) a paradisaical garden (2:8). It was unspoiled, undefiled, and uncontaminated. Because there was no death in the garden (Rom. 5:12), poisonous and harmful plants and animals would have been absent. All creatures, including Adam and Eve, were vegetarians, so there was no predation (Gen. 1:29–30). Likewise, in the absence of death, natural disasters, such as earthquakes, tornadoes, hurricanes, and tsunamis would have been unknown. (If any of these catastrophes or harmful creatures existed, it would not have been a paradise!) Moreover, clothes for warmth and protection were unnecessary for the first couple (2:25). Because God planted the garden Himself (2:8), food was bountiful and available merely by harvesting it (2:16). Adam and Eve's only responsibility was to tend and care for the garden (2:15). They didn't even have to water it (2:10).

Unfortunately, paradise was lost. Today's world is the antithesis of original creation in virtually every respect. Natural disasters are frequent. People toil for food and battle pestilence, disease, poisonous plants, and harmful animals. Fire, drought, and disease destroy plants and animals. Animals prey on one another and are crippled and killed by plagues and starvation. As the poet Alfred, Lord Tennyson put it, nature is "red in tooth and claw."[2]

What transformed the primeval, idyllic garden into today's blood-stained battleground where plants, animals, and people struggle against each other in order to survive? The Bible explains this transition in context of the fall.

When God created Adam and placed him in the garden of Eden, He told him he was free to eat any food in the garden except the fruit of one particular tree. This was a test of faith and obedience for Adam. He had a free will to choose to obey or disobey God, and God warned him of the consequences of disobedience. Adam would be punished if he ate the forbidden fruit, and death would enter the world (Gen. 2:16–17). Nevertheless, Adam and Eve disobeyed God and ate the fruit. As a result of this sin, death and decay entered the world (Gen. 3:3, 5, 22; Rom. 5:12), and the first couple was banished from the garden—a literal and symbolic picture of mankind's estrangement from God due to the fall (Gen. 3:23). Henceforth the human race would be infected with a "sin nature," an inherited tendency to engage in sinful activities contrary to God's will.[3]

The effects of the fall were not limited to humanity. Although nature itself did not fall, it was nevertheless "cursed." This is described in Genesis 3:17–19:

> "Cursed is the ground because of you [Adam];
>   through painful toil you will eat of it
>   all the days of your life.
> It will produce thorns and thistles for you,
>   and you will eat the plants of the field.
> By the sweat of your brow
>   you will eat your food
>   until you return to the ground,
>   since from it you were taken;
>   for dust you are
>   and to dust you will return."

As this passage reveals, Adam and Eve's fall into sin and resultant curse on nature triggered a major change in the relationship between humans and nature. This has played out in two distinct ways.

And Now People Exploit Nature

The fall alienated Homo sapiens from the rest of creation. It destroyed the harmonious relationship with nature that the first couple enjoyed in the garden of Eden. Eventually, even the animals Adam named and loved began to fear the human race (Gen. 9:2). All this set into motion an intrinsic exploitive behavior that became pervasive throughout the entire family of man. Since the fall, mankind has shown little concern for the welfare of his physical environment—the land, water, and air—or for the survival of other created life. Theologian Eric Charles Rust commented on this in *Nature: Garden or Desert*:

> Man, created to live in a garden, finds himself in a wilderness. . . . Instead of walking humbly with God, peaceably with his fellows, and as a steward of his natural environment, he takes the road of arrogance, selfishness, and greed. . . . Possessing the divine gift to subdue [rule] the earth, he seeks the way of arrogant overlordship and greedy exploitation. His alienation from God brings alienation from nature. . . . But nature is responsive, and it hits back at man. By their sin men have lost their true relationship to the natural order, and the natural order itself becomes perverted. . . . The idyllic possibilities in the divine intention have been lost, and man wanders as an alien in his world because he is alienated from his Creator.[4]

Let's explore how this exploitive behavior and alienation from God further affected mankind's relationship with nature.

And Nature Suffers

God has not told us exactly why nature was cursed and suffers because of human sin, but it makes perfect sense. Many scientists, theologians, and Christian apologists have argued that God created the cosmos—and the earth in particular—to support human life. As theologian and philosopher William Lane Craig said, "The entire universe and its history are fine-tuned from its inception with incredible precision to produce man on earth."[5] If God designed the earth with the human race in mind and placed Adam and Eve in a perfect natural environment specially prepared for them—and put nature under their management—it would be incongruous for nature to be unaffected when Adam and Eve rebelled against God, opened the door for death and decay to enter the world, and were expelled from the garden as part of their punishment. Nature suffers the consequences of the fall, and there is ample biblical and observational evidence that human sin continues to despoil nature. To the present day, human greed, self-indulgence, and indifference creates pollution, destroys natural habitats, and exterminates wild species of plants and animals.

Nowhere is the direct link between human sin and its devastating consequences on nature more profoundly and expansively demonstrated than the worldwide flood. Because "the Lord saw how great man's wickedness on the earth had become, and that every inclination of the thoughts of his heart was only evil all the time" (Gen. 6:5), God destroyed all life, including all people, plants, and animals—except those He called to the ark.

Unfortunately, even after God had purged the earth with worldwide floodwaters, humans continued to sin and nature continued to suffer as a result. Throughout Jewish history, the fate of the land was often interwoven with the behavior and spiritual life of the Israelites (see Jer. 9:12–14; 7:16–20).

Moses wrote in Deuteronomy 11:13–17:

> So if you faithfully obey the commands I am giving you today—to love the Lord your God and to serve him with all your heart and with all your soul—then I will send rain on your land in its season, both autumn and spring rains, so that you may gather in your grain, new wine and oil. I will provide grass in the fields for your cattle, and you will eat and be satisfied.
>
> Be careful, or you will be enticed to turn away and worship other gods and bow down to them. Then the Lord's anger will burn against you, and he will shut the heavens so that it will not rain and the ground will yield no produce, and you will soon perish from the good land the Lord is giving you."

In a similar way, the prophet Hosea warned Israel:

Hear the word of the LORD, you Israelites,
    because the LORD has a charge to bring
    against you who live in the land:
"There is no faithfulness, no love,
    no acknowledgment of God in the land.
There is only cursing, lying and murder,
    stealing and adultery;
    they break all bounds,
    and bloodshed follows bloodshed.
Because of this the land mourns,
    and all who live in it waste away;
    the beasts of the field and the birds of the air
    and the fish of the sea are dying." (4:1–3)

Time and again, God warned the Israelites that their behavior would directly affect the quality of the land. When the Jews broke God's covenant, the land suffered. The psalmist lamented:

He turned rivers into a desert,
    flowing springs into thirsty ground,
    and fruitful land into a salt waste,
    because of the wickedness of those who lived there.
                    (Ps. 107:33–34)

Elsewhere, speaking through the prophet Jeremiah, God said, "I brought you into a fertile land to eat its fruit and rich produce. But you came and defiled my land and made my inheritance detestable" (Jer. 2:7). Consequently, Jeremiah wrote that the land was parched and the grass in the fields was withered, and because "those who live in it are wicked, the animals and birds have perished" (12:4).

Similarly, the prophet Joel warned of Judah's coming judgment, but in this case it would be in the form of agricultural disaster due to a plague of locusts and drought. However, the latter part of Joel speaks of a future when God will restore Judah and Jerusalem, including the land and its wild animals:

> Be not afraid, O land;
>   be glad and rejoice.
> Surely the LORD has done great things.
> Be not afraid, O wild animals,
> For the open pastures are becoming green.
> The trees are bearing their fruit;
> The fig tree and the vine yield their riches. (2:21–22)

The biblical record also reveals that God's judgment came upon other nations who abused nature. The prophet Habakkuk reported that the Babylonians' downfall was vindicated in part because "you cut down the forests of Lebanon . . . [and] you terrified the wild animals you caught in your traps" (Hab. 2:17 NLT; see also 2 Kings 19:23). In the final judgment at the end times, the Bible reveals that God's judgment and punishment for mankind's rebellion and sin will include "those who destroy the earth" (Rev. 11:18).

The Good Land

In spite of the curse God placed on creation because of Adam's rebellion, nature after the fall remained a place of beauty, solace, serenity, and wonder—and a blessing from God to the human race. Nowhere does the Bible reveal this with more passion and delight than in its description of Israel's "Promised Land."

The land God gave the new Jewish nation when He delivered them from slavery in Egypt was a "good and spacious land . . . flowing with milk and honey" (Exod. 3:8). Moses further described it as,

> a good land—a land with streams and pools of water, with
> springs flowing in the valleys and hills; a land with wheat and

barley, vines and fig trees, pomegranates, olive oil and honey; a
land where bread will not be scarce and you will lack nothing;
a land where the rocks are iron and you can dig copper out of
the hills. (Deut. 8:7–9)

Elsewhere Moses spoke of the Promised Land as "a land of mountains
and valleys that drinks rain from heaven. It is a land the LORD your God
cares for; the eyes of the LORD . . . are continually on it from the beginning of the year to its end" (Deut. 11:11–12).

These passages not only describe a land that was abundant in natural
beauty and natural resources, but a land God valued. And, as we'll explore in a later chapter, God entrusted the Israelites to care for and manage the land, just as He instructed Adam and all other peoples.

The land—nature—still sustains the human race. We have a right to
use it, but like the Israelites, we are instructed to manage and care for it
until the time—at the end of the present age—when nature returns to
a paradisaical, pre-fall state. Then perfect harmony will return between
people and nature. Before this can happen, however, both the human race
and nature must experience redemption. This brings us to the next step in
developing a theology of nature.

CHAPTER SEVEN

REDEMPTION

God's Plan for the Restoration of Nature, Both in the Here and Now and in the Eschatological Future

Try to imagine a future, renewed earth where nature exists in a state of perfect harmony among God, people, animals, plants, and the land. A world set free from sin, suffering, evil, and natural disasters. A world of unimaginable sights, soothing sounds, sweet-scented smells, boundless textures, and perhaps even new kinds of colors. A world of peace. For people like me, who revel in walks in the woods, who thrill at even fleeting glimpses of deer and fox, and who would love nothing more than to scratch between the ears of wolf and bear, such a future earth is indescribably exciting to anticipate. *The people of God are going to experience this.*

This regenerated earth will be a material, physical, sensory world—not merely the haunt of people's immaterial souls. As theologian H. Paul Santmire explained, "The wilderness will remain, to be sure, for God also loves the alligators and the mountain lions and wills their fulfillment. But the dream of a wilderness without darkness and violence and pain will come true."[1]

What will bring about this future "new earth"? The dual redemption of the human race and nature. Let's explore how this comes about.

Redemption of the Human Race

We saw in the previous chapter that God created nature "very good" (Gen. 1:31). It was a place of pristine beauty and unspoiled perfection.

There were no natural disasters, predation, weeds, or thorns, and the first couple's only responsibility was to take care of the garden—prefiguring God's instruction to all mankind to be stewards over nature (as we'll explore in the next chapter). Unfortunately, because of human disobedience and subsequent rebellion against God set in motion by Adam and Eve, people became estranged from God through sin. This affected nature. Mankind's original harmonious relationship with nature was perverted, and enmity developed between the human race and the natural world. This culminated in the birth of an intrinsic exploitive behavior pervasive in all people and societies. Over the millennia, worldwide environmental exploitation and degradation increased as human technology increased and societies continued to fail to accept the stewardship responsibilities God had ordained.

So, the human race has a problem—which nature shares. If mankind is separated from God, guilty of sin, and deserving punishment, how can people be reconciled to God and reestablish the fellowship they once enjoyed? In addition, since nature suffers because of human sin, how can it return to its former, pre-fall state? The answer is found in the biblical teaching on redemption: God's plan for mankind's deliverance from enslavement to sin and nature's deliverance from the curse.

The Bible teaches that in humanity's fallen state, people are totally unable to reach out to God. The apostle Paul explained in Romans 8:7 that "the sinful mind is hostile to God. It does not submit to God's law, nor can it do so." Thus, for the human race to be reconciled to God, God had to take the initial step. He did this through Jesus Christ. Out of His immeasurable love for people, God came to earth as the incarnate Son in order to reconcile fallen humanity to Himself. This is called the "atonement."

The atonement entails the removal (or covering) of human sin and death by the substitutionary sacrifice of Jesus Christ on the cross (Rom. 5:8; 8:1–2; 1 Cor. 15:21–22). Jesus, the "second Adam," undid the damage caused by the first Adam—estrangement from God. Instead of guilty people making payment (redemption) for their sins, Jesus—God Himself—did it for us (Mark 10:45). This opened the door for reconciliation between God and the human race. Through Jesus Christ, we stand before God "justified." That is, on the basis of Christ's sacrifice for our sins, we are accounted righteous in God's eyes (Rom. 3:22). Just as sin became imputed to all people through Adam, Jesus' righteousness is imputed to all people who accept Him as their personal Lord and Savior (John 3:16; Rom. 5:12–21).

Redemption of Nature

Because nature's plight (the curse) is bound to mankind's plight (the fall), nature's redemption depends upon mankind's redemption (Rom. 8:19–21). Thus, when Jesus died for the sins of the world, it opened the door for the future redemption (renewal) of nature. The apostle Paul writes in Colossians 1 that through Jesus Christ God reconciled "to himself *all things*, whether things on earth or things in heaven, by making peace through his blood, shed on the cross" (v. 20, emphasis added). In other words, mankind's salvation provides the framework by which nature can be restored. Dr. Santmire said it this way: "Christ is the royal minister God sends to redeem creation, . . . [and] the royal minister God sends to inaugurate the new creation."[2]

Historically, the church has focused on the salvation of people. Nature is usually viewed as merely the backdrop, the stage on which the human drama of redemption plays out. Seldom is nature's role in redemption—and its place in the eschatological future—more than a minor consideration.

The biblical fact, however, is that not only mankind but also the entire physical world waits to be redeemed. Not because nature itself fell, but because "Man's sin against God pulled nature down along with man."[3] Cursed nature is an innocent victim of bad human choices. Thus, the removal of nature's curse is directly related to mankind's redemption; our redemption initiates nature's redemption.

God's creative work did not end with Genesis 1. The Old and New Testaments teach that there will be a future age when nature will return to a pristine state *here on earth* that will be similar, if not the same, as the garden of Eden before the fall (Isa. 51:3; Ezek. 36:35; Rom. 8:19–21). Creation does not cease to exist—it will not be annihilated—rather it will be restored and renewed.[4] In other words, just as God renews our mortal bodies at the resurrection rather than creating new bodies (Rom. 8:11; 1 Cor. 15:35–53), so the first creation will not be destroyed but renewed. This is all part of God's redemptive plan. Nature's curse will be forever removed (Rev. 22:3–5), and there will be a redeemed new heaven and new earth that will last forever (Isa. 65:17–25; Rev. 21:1).[5]

Whether this renewed earth arises at the return of Christ or a thousand years later at the end of the millennial kingdom (in which case, the millennium would be a transitional phase between the old earth and the new earth) is open to debate and not important here. What is important is that this "new creation will be the end of the 'dark side' of the first creation. All the chaotic elements of nature will be put to rest."[6] Here's how the Bible describes it.

God told the prophet Isaiah, "Behold, I will create new heavens and a new earth" (Isa. 65:17). Earlier in his book, Isaiah gave an enticing glimpse of what this new earth will be like (or a prelude to it, depending on your view of the millennial kingdom). Most noticeable is the harmony that will exist between people and animals—and among wild animals themselves:

> In that day the wolf and the lamb will live together;
> the leopard and the goat will be at peace.
> Calves and yearlings will be safe among lions,
> and a little child will lead them all.
> The cattle will graze among bears.
> Cubs and calves will lie down together.
> And lions will eat grass as the livestock do.
> Babies will crawl safely among poisonous snakes.
> Yes, a little child will put its hand in a nest of deadly snakes
> and pull it out unharmed.
> Nothing will hurt or destroy in all my holy mountain.

And as the waters fill the sea,
>   so the earth will be filled with people who know the Lord.
>   (11:6–9 NLT; also see 35; 65:17–25)

The prophet Ezekiel reported that this redeemed nature would be on planet earth. He spoke of a river that will flow "east through the desert into the Jordan Valley, where it enters the Dead Sea. The waters of this stream will heal the salty waters of the Dead Sea and make them fresh and pure. . . . Fish will abound in the Dead Sea, for its waters will be healed" (47:8–9 NLT). Unless God creates another Dead Sea on another earth, this prophecy will be fulfilled here on planet (new) earth.

In the book of Romans, Paul also speaks of a renewed or recreated earth and explicitly relates it to redeemed humanity:

> Yet what we suffer now is nothing compared to the glory he [God] will give us later. For all creation is waiting eagerly for that future day when God will reveal who his children really are. Against its will, everything on earth was subjected to God's curse. All creation anticipates the day when it will join God's children in glorious freedom from death and decay. For we know that all creation has been groaning as in the pains of childbirth right up to the present time. And even we Christians, although we have the Holy Spirit within us as a foretaste of future glory, also groan to be released from pain and suffering. We, too, wait anxiously for that day when God will give us our full rights as his children, including the new bodies he has promised us. (8:18–23 NLT)

Verse 20 reminds us that nature was cursed against its will. In light of Genesis 3:17, it's obvious this occurred at the fall. Thus, nature waits "eagerly" for its release from the curse ("death and decay"). This will come about fully in the future new heaven and earth when human redemption is completed and perfected (Rom. 8:19, 23).

Redemption Begins Now!

When Jesus taught about the kingdom of heaven (or "kingdom of God," which is the same thing), He referred to it in two ways. First, there will be a future, eschatological kingdom at the end of this age. This is the new heaven and earth discussed above (e.g., Matt. 8:11). But Jesus also taught that the kingdom of heaven entered history through His own person and ministry (see Matt. 4:17; 11:11–12; 12:28; 21:43; Luke 17:20–21). This phase of the kingdom of heaven exists in the present cosmos, and Christians enter into it the moment they become saved (John 3:3). In other words, although the kingdom of heaven will not be fully established until our resurrected bodies enter the new heaven and earth, our redemption nevertheless begins in *this* world.

It is absolutely crucial that Christians recognize this as they work to develop a biblical theology of nature and to establish environmental ethics. Here's why.

When we become Christians—saved by Christ and adopted into God's kingdom—God expects us to put into practice the moral values and behaviors and spiritual principles outlined in the Sermon on the Mount and elsewhere in Scripture. We should begin this immediately upon our conversion, upon entering the kingdom of heaven. We don't wait until we go to heaven to live a Christian life. Likewise, since the redemption of nature is bound to our redemption, we should put into practice God's divinely ordained stewardship principles while on *this* earth (we'll examine ways to do this in chapter 13). Christians are not to be idle, waiting for the future redemption of nature and doing nothing now to protect it from abuse. Such a posture is not only dishonoring to God who created and cares for nature, but it opposes the essence of our own redemption. We are to live as redeemed people *now*. Professor Seven Bouma-Prediger sums this well:

> Christian eschatology is earth-affirming. Because the earth
> will not be burned up but rather purified as in a refiner's fire

[see note 4], we can act with confidence that our actions today are not for naught. Because we yearn for a renewed heaven and earth, we can work in expectation that our faithful deeds here and now [including caring for creation] will be gathered up in the eschaton.[7]

Let me put this another way. Paul reminds us in Romans 6:8 that if we died with Christ (died to our old nature upon receiving salvation) we will also live with Him—right now. Just as Jesus was resurrected from the grave, so too are believers, upon receiving Christ, raised to a new quality of moral and spiritual life—right now (2 Cor. 5:17). Christians call this being "born again" (John 3:3). Upon receiving Jesus as Lord and Savior, we are immediately redeemed and are expected to reflect our new birth. We are empowered by the Holy Spirit to resist sin and obey God. Granted, believers will not experience perfect redemption until the future new heaven and new earth where sin is completely destroyed, and neither will nature. Nevertheless, because redemption begins the moment we are saved, we are to do our best to start living godly, obedient lives. Likewise, because nature's redemption is bound to human redemption, we are called to exercise stewardship responsibilities *now*.

Francis Schaeffer, writing during the heyday of the environmental movement, explained that Christians should be looking for "substantial" healing right now in every area that is affected by the fall.[8] In terms of our relationship with nature, he wrote: "The Christian who believes the Bible should be the man [or woman] who—with God's help and in the power of the Holy Spirit—is treating nature now in the direction of the way nature will be [in the future]."[9]

Again, it's worth repeating that nature's final and perfect healing will take place in the future new earth. This will occur after Satan and his minions are cast into the lake of fire and evil is vanquished forever (Rev. 20:7–21:1). This will be God's work, not ours. But in the meantime, just as we Christians work to achieve personal and cultural transformation on earth now, so should we fulfill our stewardship responsibilities as part of the redemption process on earth now. Francis Schaeffer drove this point home in his book *Pollution and Death of Man*:

> God's calling to the Christian now, and to the Christian community, in the area of nature—just as it is in the area of personal Christians living in true spirituality—is that we should exhibit a substantial healing here and now, between man and nature and nature and itself, as far as Christians can bring it to pass.[10]

We Have a Choice

In the area of redemption, the church corporately—and Christians individually—can choose to focus entirely on that portion of the doctrine that concerns only people, or they can focus on both the redemption of people *and* nature. Those who choose the former will probably fail to accept stewardship responsibilities over nature. This choice amounts to disobedience because it ignores God's stewardship mandate. Generally, this has been the case throughout church history. As a result, mankind's intrinsic exploitive behavior has dominated most Christians' and non-Christians' relationship with nature, and nature has suffered the consequences. Wilkinson said it well: "Unless our understanding of redemption extends to our stewardship of the earth, it is incomplete; and without redeemed persons, humanity will only destroy the rich and beautiful planet it inhabits."[11]

On the other hand, if Christians recognize nature's place in human redemption and understand that Christ's atoning work includes the redemption of nature as well as people, they will proactively respond to potential harm to the environment and accept stewardship responsibilities. The following chart illustrates this conclusion.

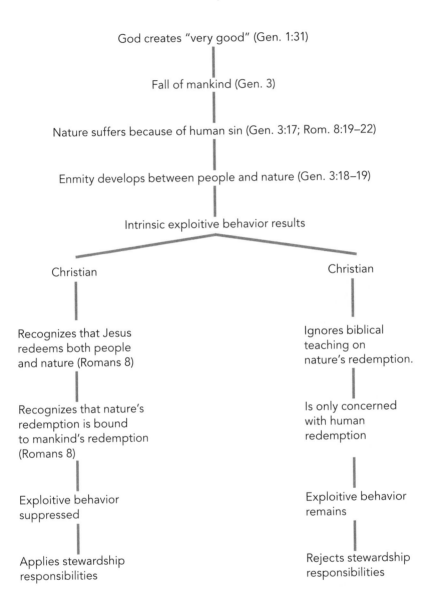

Redemption

God creates "very good" (Gen. 1:31)

Fall of mankind (Gen. 3)

Nature suffers because of human sin (Gen. 3:17; Rom. 8:19–22)

Enmity develops between people and nature (Gen. 3:18–19)

Intrinsic exploitive behavior results

Christian | Christian

Recognizes that Jesus redeems both people and nature (Romans 8) | Ignores biblical teaching on nature's redemption.

Recognizes that nature's redemption is bound to mankind's redemption (Romans 8) | Is only concerned with human redemption

Exploitive behavior suppressed | Exploitive behavior remains

Applies stewardship responsibilities | Rejects stewardship responsibilities

I've mentioned several times in previous chapters that God has commissioned the human race to be His stewards or caretakers over nature. We can now examine the passages that teach this.

CHAPTER EIGHT

STEWARDSHIP

*God Instructs the Family of Man to
Be His Caretakers over Creation*

The political landscape in America today has caused many Christians to associate the word *environmentalist* with someone who is more concerned about protecting spotted owls and redwood trees than creating jobs and acquiring energy independence. They imagine all environmentalists as tree-hugging liberals who are opposed to any economic development that may even slightly damage nature or threaten wildlife. Similarly, non-Christian environmentalists typically pigeonhole all Christians as gun-toting, tight-fisted conservatives who would sacrifice any habitat and any wild creature to fuel the furnace of economic growth.

Of course both camps are guilty of hyperbole and ignorance. It seems to me that the solution to this hostility is for both Christians and non-Christian environmentalists to understand what the Bible actually teaches about environmental stewardship.

The Challenge

In chapter 4, I related a conversation I had with a Christian friend who is critical of environmentalism. In one of our last discussions, I asked him this question: "What if God *told us* to take care of nature?" In other words, what if God instructed people to protect and manage wildlife, as well as forests, rivers, the land, and air? A simple and straightforward question—but one he refused to answer. The reason was obvious. If my friend admitted that God instructed the human race to care for and manage His creation, he would have to reevaluate his attitude toward environmental activism in light of biblical truth. He was unwilling to do that. If God instructed the human race to care for creation, who can argue against that? The task would become, how do we do it?

This is a challenge that all Christians who claim allegiance to God and accept the Bible as their source of authority should willingly seek to answer. As this book repeatedly demonstrates, the view that God does not mind if people exploit and despoil nature cannot be substantiated in Scriptures. The fact is Christians (and all people) are indisputably called by God to be His stewards over creation. What is the biblical model of stewardship? What does a steward do? This is the subject of the present chapter.

The Biblical Model

Before we explore biblical stewardship, we need to examine a passage in Scripture. It *appears* to contradict my assertion that God has *not* given the human race carte blanche to use nature as they choose without any regard for other created life. Critics almost universally use this passage to support their claim that the Bible promotes an exploitive attitude toward nature. I'm referring to Genesis 1:27–28, especially as it's worded in the Authorized or King James Version:

> So God created man in his own image, in the image of God created he him; male and female created he them.
>
> And God blessed them, and God said unto them, Be fruitful, and multiply, and replenish the earth, and subdue it: and have dominion over the fish of the sea, and over the fowl of the air, and over every living thing that moveth upon the earth.

What, exactly, does the Bible mean when it exhorts the human race to "subdue" the earth and to have "dominion" over nature? Does this passage allow or even encourage people to misuse nature for any reason? No, it doesn't.

When we come upon a passage in Scripture that appears to contradict the overall biblical teachings on a subject, although we may not know exactly what that passage means, we can know what it *doesn't* mean. It cannot mean anything that contradicts the rest of the Bible's teaching on the topic. In other words, if at first glance the interpretation of Genesis 1:27–28 appears to contradict the rest of what the Bible teaches on environmental stewardship, the aberrant interpretation is incorrect and should be discarded. In light of this, let's examine Genesis 1:27–28 and determine what it *doesn't* mean. This in turn will shed light on what the passage *does* mean.

A Lesson in Hermeneutics

The first step toward understanding the meaning of Genesis 1:27–28 is to review a basic principle of *hermeneutics*. Hermeneutics refers to interpretative techniques that are applied to literary texts, in particular the Bible. Although several important principles are associated with proper hermeneutics, one in particular is relevant to Genesis 1:27–28.

This fundamental rule of biblical hermeneutics is to interpret any passage within context of surrounding passages as well as within context of other passages that speak on the same topic. This is crucial because a single passage in the Bible usually doesn't provide the full meaning or total teaching on a particular subject. Many doctrines in Scripture require a systematic study of numerous related passages. The doctrine of the Trinity is a classic example. No single passage in the Bible adequately defines this doctrine—indeed, the word *Trinity* is not even in the Bible. Yet when we examine the numerous passages revealing the nature of God, we find that the Father, the Son, and the Holy Spirit all possess identical attributes. Thus, the one God (Deut. 6:4) eternally exists as Father, Son, and Holy Spirit—the Trinity.[1]

The closest *related* passages to Genesis 1:27–28 are found in Genesis chapter 2. This chapter provides additional details about the creation of the first man and woman and the physical environment in which they lived. We'll examine the passages in Genesis 2 that are related to Genesis 1:27–28.

The LORD God formed the man from the dust of the ground and breathed into his nostrils the breath of life, and the man became a living being.

Now the LORD God had planted a garden in the east, in Eden; and there he put the man he had formed. (2:7–8)

The LORD God took the man and put him in the Garden of Eden to work it and take care of it. (2:15)

So the LORD God caused the man to fall into a deep sleep; and while he was sleeping, he took one of the man's ribs and closed up the place with flesh. Then the LORD God made a woman from the rib he had taken out of the man, and he brought her to the man. (2:21–22)

Genesis 2:7–8 relates that God created a garden in Eden and placed Adam, the first man, in it. Genesis 2:15 adds that Adam was instructed to "take care of" the garden. Only later, after these events occurred, did God create Eve, the first woman (vv. 21–22). In light of this chronology, it's important to understand that God's instructions to subdue the earth and to have dominion over nature were given *after* Eve was created and while the couple was living in the garden of Eden. How do we know this? Because the so-called dominion instructions were given to *both* Adam and Eve (Gen. 1:27–28). Thus, since Eve was created after Adam was placed in the garden—and before their banishment from Eden (Gen. 3)—the "subdue" and "dominion" instructions had to have been given while the couple resided in the garden.

Why is this important? Because the harsh sounding words *subdue* and *dominion* in Genesis 1:28 are softened and qualified due to the garden setting where the instructions were given. The natural environment in which Adam and Eve lived (before the fall) was a *paradise*. It was free of thorns, thistles, and ferocious animals. It's preposterous to think that the injunction to subdue the earth and to have dominion over nature had anything to do with battling or destroying nature. There was nothing to conquer in the garden of Eden! Fulfilling Adam and Eve's nutritional and other physical needs in the garden would not have necessitated toil and hardship. The couple could effortlessly select their food from the abundant plant life surrounding them (Gen. 2:9, 16). Whatever *subdue* and *dominion* mean in Genesis 1:28, they do not carry a despotic connotation or suggest the freedom to recklessly and harmfully exploit nature.

With this in mind, it's understandable why modern translations, such as the New American Standard Bible and New International Version, have replaced the world *dominion* in Genesis 1:28 in the King James Version with *rule*:

> God blessed them; and God said to them, "Be fruitful and multiply, and fill the earth, and subdue it; and rule over the fish of the sea and over the birds of the sky and over every living thing that moves on the earth." (NASB)

Modern translators have access to many more ancient manuscripts than the compilers of the King James Version (originally printed in 1611). The word *rule* reflects a more precise understanding of what the Hebrew word translated *dominion* in the King James Version actually means. When Genesis 1:27–28 is harmonized in context with Genesis 2, we see a more accurate interpretation of what "subdue the earth" and "have dominion [rule] over nature" actually implies.

People who claim that Genesis 1:28 provides a license from God to exploit nature solely for human pleasure fail to heed the cardinal hermeneutical principle of interpreting a single passage within context of related passages as well as the whole biblical teaching on the topic. Critics select Genesis 1:28 (often quoting the King James Version) as a primary proof-text and disregard the host of other passages that reveal what God actually means by His instructions to mankind to subdue the earth and to have dominion (rule) over nature. Santmire explained:

The so-called biblical idea of dominion as most of us have been taught it . . . is only dimly reflective of the actual historical biblical motif in its original setting, and in the pre-modern theological traditions. Other biblical and classical theological motifs, moreover, which balanced and delimited the biblical idea of dominion, have been over-looked by many modern popular and scholarly interpreters of the Bible.[2]

Henlee H. Barnette, Christian author and ethicist, agreed:

This passage [Genesis 1:28] has been cited by some writers . . . as the source from which the Jews and Christians derive the concept of an anthropocentric universe and legitimation for despoiling the earth. Whatever truth there may be to this charge, to make Genesis 1:28 the root of the current environmental problem is preposterous. Unfortunately, this simplistic explanation has received wide acceptance in academic circles and the press. To hold that Genesis 1:28 provides a blank check for man to ruthlessly exploit nature is bad hermeneutics. When man is viewed from the perspective of the total teaching of the Bible, one gets a radically different view of him and his relationship to nature.[3]

So, *subdue* and *dominion*, as they relate to mankind's involvement with nature, do not mean that people have the right to exploit and despoil God's creation. Rather the words imply that people have a stewardship or caretaker's role over nature. I like the way John Stott put it:

The dominion God has given us is delegated, responsible and cooperative; . . . it is intended to express the same sustaining care of the environment as its Creator's; and . . . far from exploiting the earth and its creatures, we are to use them in such a way as to be accountable to God and to serve others. . . .

The dominion God has given humankind is a conscientious and caring stewardship which involves the husbanding of the earth's resources. It would be ludicrous to suppose that God first created the earth and then handed it over to us to destroy it.[4]

Dominion in the sense of absolute authority is only the prerogative of God—whether it concerns nature or anything else. People are custodians; they do not own the earth. As Francis Schaeffer pointed out, "Man has dominion over the 'lower' orders of creation, but he is not sovereign over them. Only God is the Sovereign Lord, and the lower orders are to be used with this truth in mind. Man is not using his own possessions."[5]

Other writers make the same point. Professor C. F. D. Moule stated it this way:

Man is placed in the world by God to be its lord. He is meant to have dominion over it and to use it . . . but only for God's sake, only like Adam in paradise, cultivating it for the Lord. As soon as he begins to use it selfishly, . . . instantly the ecological balance is upset and nature begins to groan.[6]

Likewise, Barnette:

The biblical view of man is that of a "keeper," caretaker, custodian, curator of the *oikos*, the household earth. Man is God's deputy to oversee, direct, and care for the environment. "Steward" is the New Testament term for this role of man in relation to the natural order. It refers to the manager or administrator of an estate. The first requirement of a steward is faithfulness, because he handles that which belongs to another [i.e., God].[7]

Finally, eminent scholar and theologian Carl F. H. Henry declared,

The conservation and preservation of nature are Christian imperatives. . . . The view of Genesis, that man is the divinely delegated steward (even if in this respect some Christians, like non-Christians, have shown a callous indifference to environmental concerns) is not the source of ecological insensitivity.[8]

If Schaeffer's, Moule's, Barnette's, and Henry's assessments of what the Bible teaches with regard to mankind's stewardship role in nature are correct, there is a contradiction between how non-Christian environmentalists (and, unfortunately, many Christians) interpret the Bible and what it actually says. The Bible teaches stewardship, not exploitation.

With an accurate interpretation of the controversial words *subdue* and *dominion* as they relate to Genesis 1:27–28 and harmonize with Genesis 2, we can now explore exactly what a steward does.

What Does a Steward Do?

The Bible illustrates the concept of stewardship in several places. In Luke 12:42, Jesus described a "faithful and wise manager" as one "whom the master puts in charge of his servants." (The NLT says one "to whom the master gives the responsibility of managing his household and feeding his family.") Perhaps the best illustration of the biblical model of stewardship is found in the Parable of the Talents (Matt. 25:14–30). This parable speaks about a man who went on a long journey and entrusted his possessions to his slaves. He gave "talents" (large sums of money) to three of his slaves (vv. 14–15). Upon the master's return, he confronted the slaves to see how well they invested his money. Two of the slaves doubled the amount entrusted to them and were rewarded for their faithfulness. But the third slave failed to use his talent wisely and was severely punished.

In like manner, nature belongs to God, but He appointed the human race to be His stewards. Our responsibility is to care for the owner's (God's) property (Lev. 25:23). And like the slaves in the Parable of the Talents, people will be held accountable for how well they perform this task that the Master entrusted to them.

This model of stewardship comes to life in Genesis 2:15: "The LORD God took the man and put him in the Garden of Eden to work it and take care of it." The Hebrew word in this passage for "work" is *abad*, which is most often translated as "serve," though it may also be translated "till" or "cultivate." Similarly, the Hebrew word for "take care of" is *shamar*, a word that implies watching over something, guarding and preserving it. The Hebrew meaning of these two words clearly instructs the first couple to watch over and tend the garden. Neither usage allows for plunder, exploitation, or abuse.

Adam's caretaker role in nature was further illustrated when God instructed him to name the animals in Genesis 2:19. By relegating this authority to Adam, God not only demonstrated his personal interest and concern for the animals He created, but also His desire for Adam to take responsibility for them. (By analogy, when people name their pets and when zoos name the animals under their care, they demonstrate their affection and assume the responsibility to take care of them.)

A similar stewardship role was later given to Noah. God commanded Noah to preserve in the ark a genetic stock of two of *every* kind of living creature (Gen. 6:19). This command was not qualified, so it must have included so-called "vermin" and predators as well as animals profitable to people. Thus, Noah's stewardship responsibilities included all creatures, not just those that serve people.

God's stewardship charge continued with the rise of the Jewish nation. Thousands of years before modern environmental laws, God required the Hebrews to curb pollution by properly disposing of waste products (Deut. 23:12–13) and to rest from sowing their fields every seventh year in order to restore the soil (Lev. 25:2–4). (This was also to allow poor people and *wild animals* to eat what was left, according to Exodus 23:11.) God taught the Hebrews not to eat the fruit of newly planted trees for five years until the trees had time to mature (Lev. 19:23–25). During the conquest of Canaan, God instructed the Israelites to use only non-fruiting trees to construct their siege machines: "Are the trees of the field people, that you should besiege them?" (Deut. 20:19).

God's divine commands for Adam to tend and care for the garden of Eden; Noah to preserve and care for the animals God would use to re-populate the earth; and the Israelites to be careful stewards of the land God provided them can be extrapolated to include the entire human race and *today's* natural world. Nowhere does the Bible teach that God's edict to care for nature was limited to just Adam in the garden or to Noah and the Israelites. In light of the numerous passages we've examined in our study, it's unarguable that the entire human race is a recipient of the stewardship mandate.

The doctrine of stewardship, applied to nature and harmonized with the correct biblical meanings of *subdue* and *dominion*, acknowledges that nature is God's property and that He delegated a caretaker's role to humanity. A steward does not own what he or she protects. With this responsibility comes accountability. As the Parable of the Talents illustrates, we will be rewarded if we perform our stewardship role well, and we can expect punishment if we don't. Church historian and theologian Geoffrey Bromiley put it like this: God "will have words of commendation for those who work for the integrity of creation and words of rebuke for those who abuse his handiwork to selfish or wicked ends."[9]

The Consequences of Poor Stewardship

Unfortunately, the human race has failed to take its stewardship responsibilities over nature seriously—and we see the consequences (the "punishment") of this everywhere across the globe: The extinction of thousands of plant and animal species; huge tracts of the earth spoiled and contaminated; air and water pollution; loss forever of scenic rivers, forests, wetlands, and other irreplaceable wild habitats. I believe, as Professor Bromiley implied, the Bible teaches that God will hold mankind accountable for this disastrous irresponsibility. Revelation 11:18 gives a grim warning of the fate of rebellious humanity that includes punishing people who "destroy the earth":

The nations were angry;
    and your wrath has come.
The time has come for judging the dead,
    and for rewarding your servants the prophets
    and your saints and those who reverence your name,
    both small and great—
    and for destroying those who destroy the earth.
                           (Rev. 11:18, emphasis added)

Commenting on this passage, Bible expositor Dr. Warren Wiersbe explained:

> Sinful man has polluted and destroyed God's wonderful creation; and he is going to pay for it. . . . Creation is for God's praise and pleasure, and man has no right to usurp that which rightfully belongs to God. . . .
>
> "[Those who] destroy the earth" refers to the rebellious earth-dwellers who will not submit to God. How ironic that these people live for the earth and its pleasures, yet at the same time are *destroying* the very earth that they worship! When man forgets that God is the Creator and he is the creature, he begins to exploit his God-given resources, and this brings destruction. Man is a steward of creation, not the owner.[10]

God always keeps His promises. Our response to His charge for the human race to be stewards over nature, however, should not be motivated just out of fear of punishment for a job poorly done. If we love God, we should make every effort to honor and protect what He considers important and of value.

CHAPTER NINE

ENVIRONMENTAL DOCTRINAL STATEMENT

A Summarization

We have examined four biblical doctrines that form the building blocks—the theological infrastructure—of an environmental doctrine. I'll summarize these four components and then synthesize them into a succinct doctrinal statement.

Creation

God is the creator, sustainer, and ruler of the universe. He is transcendent apart from nature by virtue of being the Creator; He is immanent to His creation by virtue of His omnipresence and omniscience. God created the natural laws by which nature operates and is aware of every particle of matter and every event that occurs in nature. Nature has value apart from—but not above—mankind. God loves, provides for, and has great concern for the welfare of nature. The human race was created in God's image. As such, we share certain communicable attributes of the Divine nature (although qualitatively, immeasurably less than God's). People hold a dual position in nature. On the one hand, our physical existence places us in a genuine kinship with other created life. We share the earth and depend on its natural resources for survival—just like plants and animals. On the other hand, because we were created in God's image, we are the "crown of creation." With this comes responsibilities. God gave the human race a divinely ordained stewardship role over the rest of creation (nature).

The Fall

Adam, the first human being, was placed in the garden of Eden. The garden was a paradise, and Adam and (later) Eve lived in perfect harmony with nature. God instructed Adam to tend, cultivate, and watch over the garden. Because Adam was the representative head of the human race, this decree was passed on to all future generations and included all future natural environments. Unfortunately, because Adam and Eve disobeyed God and succumbed to the temptation to sin, they were expelled from the garden. As a result, nature was "cursed"; that is, nature is no longer a garden paradise. It became contaminated, corrupted, and marred. All living things, including people, now strive to survive amidst natural disasters, disease, fire, drought, predation, and plagues. Because of this, enmity arose between nature and all subsequent generations of people. Thus, the human race became alienated from nature. The "fall of mankind" did not remove God's edict for people to be His caretakers over creation. Nevertheless, the human race failed in this responsibility and instead acquired—and still manifests—an intrinsic exploitive behavior. Just as all people individually and corporately in their societies possess a natural tendency to sin, so does the family of man exhibit a proclivity to exploit (abuse and despoil) nature for purely selfish gain. Because God decreed that the human race act as His stewards over nature, this act of disobedience and rebellion is a sin against God.

Redemption

God came to earth as the incarnate Son and was sacrificed on the cross for our redemption. Those who receive Jesus Christ as Lord and Savior are forgiven for their sins and reconciled with God. Because nature suffers the consequences of the fall of mankind (the "curse"), it too will be redeemed through Jesus Christ. Jesus' atonement opened the door, provided the framework, for the future redemption (renewal) of nature. Perfect and fully redeemed humanity and nature will not be realized until the future new heaven and new earth. Nevertheless, just as people are called to practice redemptive activities in the here and now—that is, to live according the ethical standards and principles taught in the Bible—so too are we called to exercise stewardship responsibilities in nature as part of the redemptive process going on in this present age.

Stewardship

The biblical instruction for mankind to "subdue" the earth and to have "dominion" over nature does not mean that the human race has a right to exploit and despoil nature. By applying correct hermeneutical principles to Genesis 1:28 and the related passages in Genesis 2, *subdue* and *dominion* have an explicit stewardship connotation. God assigned to the human family, beginning with Adam, the responsibility to be His custodians, His managers, over creation. We are accountable to God (like any steward) for how well we fulfill this divine mandate. People and cultures may use nature to fulfill their own nutritional, material, and energy needs. As they do so, however, God expects the human family to consider the welfare of the land and all creatures entrusted to their care. Failure to do this has resulted in—and if not curtailed will continue to result in—environmental degradation. God will hold people accountable for their failure to obey His stewardship instructions.

❖ Environmental Doctrinal Statement ❖

God created nature "very good." It has value and importance independent of and apart from the human race. God cares for and provides for nature and instructed mankind corporately to be His stewards, His custodians over creation. This includes the land, air, water, wild habitats, natural resources, and animal life (both wild and domesticated). People and their societies may use nature and natural resources for their own purposes. In pursuing this, however, they do not have a license to destructively exploit and recklessly despoil nature solely to benefit humanity. God will hold people accountable for not obeying His stewardship assignment. Environmental exploitation and abuse is disobedience to God and, therefore, sin.

With a biblical environmental doctrine established, we can now develop practical environmental ethics that are based on it. They will serve to direct the human family's corporate and individual relationship with nature and provide guidelines for environmental stewardship.

PART THREE

ENVIRONMENTAL ETHICS AND THE ROLE OF THE CHURCH

CHAPTER TEN

AMERICA'S EMERGING ECOLOGICAL CONSCIENCE

I n 1979, the waning days of the back-to-the-land movement, I moved my family to a rural community in Southern California. My wife and I wanted to raise our children alongside of goats, chickens, and an enormous, pesticide-free vegetable garden. It was a grand adventure. We all learned to milk goats. We ate goat cheese and drank goat milk. We had fresh eggs and vegetables. My kids learned to ride a horse. But the best thing that happened during that time was that my children and I became Christians (my wife was already a believer).

Shortly after I became a Christian, my pastor introduced me to the academic dean of a one-year Bible college located in the wilds of Montana— ten miles up a dirt road from the nearest *small* town. We became great friends. Like me Tom was a nature lover, and we enjoyed hiking together when I visited him in Montana and when he spent time here in Southern California. I have a particularly fond memory of a cross-country hike we took in the forest east of my home. It was not just the hike I remember; it was picking Tom's brain about theological questions. One subject that fascinated me was a class he taught at the college called "Theology of the Wilderness." It became one of the references for my master's thesis on environmental ethics and stewardship.

At the time, Tom was the only Christian I knew who shared my passion for the wilderness and understood that the Bible embraces a clearly identifiable theology of nature. This is not surprising. In the history of American environmentalism, God's perspective on environmental ethics and stewardship has seldom been considered, either by Christians or non-Christians.

Before the 1960s (with a few notable exceptions), it was rare to view nature through a moral frame of reference that stressed its value independent of human priorities. Most early advocates for environmental ethics were solitary voices "crying in the wilderness"—eccentric wilderness sages of the John Muir mold. In popular opinion, any worth that nature possessed was largely determined by how it served human needs. The transition from this utilitarian mind-set to today's increasingly sympathetic attitude that nature has value *independent* of human needs is the opening paragraph in the modern environmental movement. Sadly, Christians were not the leaders of this transformation—which helps to explain why most environmentalists continue to be non-Christians.

Romanticism

By the early nineteenth century, American writers, poets, and artists had begun to ask the question, "What is it in this new country that is distinctively American?"[1] The United States did not have a long history compared to European nations with their rich cultural heritage, ancient ruins, and Gothic cathedrals. But America did have something Europe didn't have: vast, untouched, seemingly endless wildernesses. After the Revolutionary War, this awareness began to dominate American literature and art—and it eventually spawned a new perspective on wild nature.

The seeds of an environmental conscience in America were planted by the nineteenth-century Romantics. Prior to the Romantic period (late eighteenth to mid-nineteenth centuries), the Scientific Revolution had advanced a paradigm that considered nature a vast organic machine operating according to immutable natural laws. Nature was understood in purely mechanical terms. It had no moral or spiritual significance; animals were regarded as mindless, soulless, and even without the ability to feel physical pain (which sometimes resulted in the cruel practice of vivisection). Nature was to be conquered, exploited as needed, and used solely for human pleasure, profit, and consumption.

Romanticism was a reaction against this insensitive, mechanical view of nature. The Romantics realized that mankind was becoming increasingly isolated from nature—not only physically but also spiritually—and "sought to redefine nature and man's place in the scheme of things."[2] They advanced a new paradigm of nature, one in which nature was alive, dynamic, and permeated with spiritual energy—and a path to religious experiences. The Romantics recognized the interrelatedness of all life (including Homo sapiens) and "believed that a renewed, harmonious relation to nature was the only remedy for the spiritual as well as the physical ills that marked their times."[3] They came to "identify the vitality of American life with nature" and were opposed to the trappings and technology of civilization.[4] Transcendentalists (Romanticism in America), such as Henry David Thoreau and Ralph Waldo Emerson in New England, and preservationist John Muir in the West (who called grazing sheep "hoofed Locust")—as well as many other American poets and writers—became popular spokesmen for the Romantic way of thinking about nature.

In terms of America's emerging ecological conscience, nowhere was the Romantic philosophy more influential than in the landscape painting movement that emerged out it. "Towering mountains, giant trees, and sublime wilderness landscapes had never been painted before,"[5] and people flocked to see portrayals of natural wonders they hoped someday to see with their own eyes. By the mid-nineteenth century, landscape paintings of America's natural wonders became the most popular category of art. Thomas Cole, Frederic Edwin Church, Albert Bierstadt, Thomas Moran, and other landscape painters opened people's eyes to the importance of preserving wild nature and helped to foster a new kind of pride in America by developing an identity that was grounded in our unique natural heritage. (This identity still persists, as witnessed by the thousands of Europeans and Asians who visit America's national parks every year.)

Unfortunately, however, the Romantics did not assimilate the Christian worldview. As a movement, Romanticism rejected traditional

Christian theology and ethics.[6] Rather, the Romantics identified deity with the life forces of nature or some kind of spiritual presence, making the movement theologically more in line with pantheism and animism than Christianity. Nevertheless, the Romantics, through art, poetry, and other writings, cultivated in the minds of many Americans a deeper appreciation of nature's beauty and magnificence. This new interest in wild places eventually led to the establishment of national parks, preserves, and outdoor-oriented organizations such as the Sierra Club (founded by John Muir) and the Boy Scouts. During his tenure as chief executive (1901–1909), Theodore Roosevelt promoted conservation more than any other president in American history. He designated 150 national forests, five national parks, and numerous national monuments, game preserves, and bird sanctuaries. As Christian environmentalist and theologian Loren Wilkinson pointed out, "Many of the contemporary appreciative attitudes toward nature which we now take for granted—the motives for mountain-climbing, bird-watching, or backpacking—have their origins in what we could call the 'Romantic Revolution.'"[7]

Although the Romantics and landscape artists heightened America's awareness of the recreational and "spiritual" value of nature and fueled the preservationist movement to set aside sizeable tracts of scenic, unspoiled wilderness for future generations, they nevertheless failed to establish an ethical standard that regarded nature as valuable independent of human use. Conservationists wanted to protect the aesthetic value and recreational benefits of nature, but their primary concerns were to prevent resource depletion, such as managing forests to yield maximum lumber production. Thus, America's exploitive activities remained largely unabated, even though they were cushioned by the establishment of "hands-off" tracts of wilderness areas in preserves and national parks.

The Dust Bowl

A more ecological approach to environmentalism, one that included not only conserving natural resources for economic, scenic, and recreational purposes but also for the welfare of nature itself, did not begin to emerge until the twentieth century. Many credit the beginning of this transition to the devastating effects of the Dust Bowl experience in the plains states during the 1930s.

For decades the prairie grasslands had been converted into farmland, destroying the native vegetation. In the early 1930s, the Midwest was hit with a severe drought and constant winds. Without native grasses to control wind erosion, countless millions of tons of topsoil were blown away, some of it as far as the Eastern seaboard. Thousands of farmers lost their land and migrated west—300,000 to California alone.[8] It became brutally apparent that preserving entire ecosystems was vital to the health of the land as well as the health of the people. This marked an awakening consciousness in America that people must coexist with nature and establish a system of land management that protects wildlife and plant life as well as natural resources. The science of ecology and modern environmentalism was born.

Aldo Leopold

In the mid-twentieth century, the first major spokesman to promote broad-based environmental ethics came on the scene. Aldo Leopold (1886–1948) was unarguably the foremost conservationist of the twentieth century and the first to express the need for an "ecological conscience."[9] He represented the transition from the older conservation philosophy that regarded conservation as preventing resource depletion and ensuring recreational activities and the modern ecological consciousness that stresses preserving nature for nature's sake as well as mankind's. Unlike the Romantics, who promoted an experiential, sentimental, and sometimes idealistic attitude toward nature—often in religious terms—Leopold articulated needed reforms in wildlife management and the way Americans treated the land from a scientific perspective. His famous essay, "The Land Ethic," published posthumously in *A Sand County Almanac,*[10] marked the arrival of the Age of Ecology.[11]

Aldo Leopold is considered the father of wildlife management in America. He was acutely aware that the basic weakness in wildlife conservation was that it was based entirely on economic motives. Prior to Leopold, wildlife management strategies were formulated according to the value that animals had to people. Predators, for example, were deemed valuable only to the degree that they culled old and diseased game animals (animals used for recreational hunting) and controlled rodents. Most conservationists at the time agreed that if predators killed domestic stock or too many game animals, they should be eliminated. Thus, predators had no intrinsic worth outside utilitarian considerations. Game animals, on the other hand, were of economic importance (e.g., license fees) and thus received most of the funding from wildlife management agencies.

Leopold recognized "the inadequacy of economic expediency in conservation"[12] and lamented that "there is as yet no ethic dealing with man's relation to the land and to the animals and plants which grow upon it."[13] He pointed out that human beings are members of a community of living things, and that ethics must be extended to include non-human life and even natural objects: "The land ethic simply enlarges the boundaries of the community to include soils, water, plants, and animals, or collectively: the land."[14] Leopold believed that the conservation movement of his generation would be "the embryo" of an emerging land ethic that would result in a shift in "the role of *Homo sapiens* from conqueror of the land-community to plain member and citizen of it."[15] Of course, because people were created in God's image and entrusted with stewardship responsibilities, we are more than "plain member and citizen" of the land community. Nevertheless, Leopold's belief that the conservation movement should embrace a land ethic that includes non-human life and even natural objects *is* biblically sound.

Interestingly, Leopold acknowledged that the earliest thinkers to identify the necessity of an ethical perspective toward the land, including "the animals and plants which grow upon it," were biblical characters: "Individual thinkers since the days of Ezekiel and Isaiah have asserted that the despoliation of land is not only inexpedient but wrong."[16]

Unfortunately, wilderness philosophers such as Henry David Thoreau (1817–1862), poetic spokesmen such as John Muir (1838–1914), and thoughtful oracles such as Aldo Leopold (1886–1948) failed to fully awaken public awareness to the damaging consequences to nature of human exploitation—as well as its consequences to the entire human race. It was not until the emerging environmental crisis in the early 1960s that Americans became alarmed over our rapidly deteriorating land, water, air, and wildlife resources.

Sadly, even with the passing of nearly fifty years, management decisions regarding native habitats and wildlife are often still based on economic incentives rather than what's best for the environment and its wild denizens. Case in point is the near constant battle between the lumber and ranching industries and conservationists over how best to use our national forests and other public lands. As I write this chapter, a movement is in full force to remove federal endangered species protection for gray wolves, which were introduced into Yellowstone National Park in 1995. This could open the door for trophy hunters who wish to mount wolf pelts on their den walls, as well as allow ranchers to kill wolves that occasionally prey on livestock (even though Defenders of Wildlife reimbursed ranchers whose livestock have been killed or injured by wolves).

What is needed, it seems to me, is to heed Aldo Leopold's advice and formulate a new ethical attitude toward nature that expands human ethics to the land and the plants and animals that inhabit it. The starting point for achieving this is to acknowledge the biblical teaching that other created things have inherent worth because God considers them of value and cares for them.

Although not Bible based, Aldo Leopold endorsed a model of environmental ethics that focused on the inherent worth of nature in "The Land Ethic." Commenting on this, environmental historian Donald Worster wrote:

> Ecology revealed to Leopold a new dimension in the very old notion of natural rights. . . . By the very order of nature

. . . certain inalienable rights belong to all men, but natural rights had never included the rights of nature. The ecological conscience, however, would extend these concepts to all species, even to the earth itself. . . . Unless man recognized the rights of the entire earth household, Leopold warned, he might find his own survival threatened by environmental collapse. It has happened before, as recently as the Dust Bowl years.[17]

The idea that "natural rights" should be extended "to all species, even to the earth itself" is a provocative and intriguing thought. It's worth exploring further to see if it is in harmony with biblical revelation.

Do Natural Objects Have "Rights"?

The answer to the question posed in the above subheading is *no*, particularly in light of how the term would be interpreted in neo-pagan and other nature religions (see chapter 3). Christians should never use the term "rights" in the sense that plants and animals and natural objects have equality with humans or intrinsic value beyond what God ascribes to them. Having clarified this important point, let's explore this notion in context of America's emerging ecological conscience.

Industrial, agricultural, lumber, recreational, and human health considerations have long been the primary motivation for conservation efforts in America. Cleaning up polluted lakes, rivers, and streams, for example, is as much about preserving clean drinking water and recreational fishing as it is protecting the fish. As a result, land and wildlife management has historically been human centered. Although not a fallacious argument for establishing conservation-minded ethics, it's transparently anthropocentric, and it carries an inherent weakness. Because environmental concerns are often focused on economic and land use issues, the overall welfare of nature is not always considered—unless endangered species or imperiled habitats are threatened (such as when a contractor wants to develop coastal wetlands). This leaves little room for preemptive conservation strategies designed to prevent future environmental damage in presently non-threatened habitats.

In a thought-provoking book, *Should Trees Have Standing?*,[18] University of Southern California law professor Christopher Stone suggested that natural objects be given "legal standing" in the same way as corporations, estates, railroads, and other non-sentient things. He advocated that forests, oceans, rivers, the land, and other natural objects in the environment have inherent worth and, therefore, should be recognized by our legal system as possessing rights.[19] Stone does *not* suggest that trees or other natural objects have the same rights as human beings. However, they should have access to representation in court by legal counsel, just as corporations and other legal entities. If natural objects have legal rights, a "guardian" could take an environmental offender to court on behalf of the natural object itself. A guardian, explained Stone, would be the "legal representative" of a natural object, assuring that "the environment will be represented by the most effective voice available." The guardian concept, Stone continued, "would provide the endangered natural object with what the trustee in bankruptcy provides the endangered corporation: a continuous responsibility and supervision over a period of time."[20]

Having emphasized that Christians would not use the term "rights" in describing the worth or value of plants, animals, and natural objects, I believe Stone's provocative proposal—interpreted through a biblical filter—deserves consideration. A biblical theology of nature, as developed in previous chapters, gives support to his thesis. Natural objects have value to God independent of their importance to the human race. As such, they should be protected for their own sakes—not just for their economic, recreational, or aesthetic value to people. Protecting natural objects as well as plants and animals from destructive exploitation and degradation *is* an ethical principle in harmony with God's love, provision, and concern for His creation and mankind's stewardship responsibility over nature.

The main reason I discuss Stone's suggestion that natural objects be given legal protection is that it raises two important *theological* questions.

First, is environmental exploitation sin? We looked at this briefly in an earlier chapter, but it needs to be examined more closely. We'll do this in the following chapter.

Second, assuming that Christians can (with biblical justification) extrapolate human ethics to non-human life and even natural objects, what moral principles in the Bible support it? This will be the topic of chapter 12, where I will develop an ethical basis for environmental stewardship that arises directly from moral principles taught by Jesus.

CHAPTER ELEVEN

IS ENVIRONMENTAL EXPLOITATION SIN?

A few years ago *Time* magazine carried an article on "Urban Poaching." The author quoted "wildlife officials [who] estimate that the number of poached animals matches the amount of game legally taken each year."[1] I was amazed. I knew poaching was a serious problem in some African and Asian nations, but I didn't realize it was a serious problem in the United States. The article illustrated this with several poignant examples: a black bear, which for years was a "parking-lot show" at a Pennsylvania restaurant, was shot with a crossbow for no reason. White-tailed deer are sometimes slaughtered only for their antlers. (Elk antlers, the article reported, can bring a poacher $10,000; bighorn sheep horns, $60,000!)

The heartless and illegal practice of killing animals for "fun" or profit (often leaving the carcasses where they lie) brings us back to a theological question we touched on briefly in a previous chapter: Is destructive environmental exploitation sin? To use our present example, is *illegally* killing animals (obviously a form of environmental exploitation) a sin because it violates human laws (Rom. 13:1–2), or is it also sin because unnecessarily killing creatures that God created and values *independent* of people is a sin against God?

Before we consider Bible-based environmental ethics, it's important that this issue be settled.

Some argue that environmental exploitation is sin only if and when it affects people. If it just affects nature, it's not sin. In this case, poaching would be a sin only because it violates human laws. This view is based on the fact that God gave the human race the authority to "rule" over nature (Gen. 1:28), and that people are more valuable than other life forms (Ps. 8:5–8). Consequently, the reasoning goes, ecological and environmental abuse can legitimately be called sin only if it affects humans. It should be noted, however, that even by this criterion some forms of environmental exploitation would still be sin. Air, water, and land pollution not only harm nature but also people. In fact, it could be argued that killing wild animals unnecessarily is also sin because it diminishes the quality and enjoyment of non-hunters' wilderness experiences.

Be this as it may, are people who claim that abusing nature is morally wrong only if it harms people correct—or is it immoral to abuse nature even if it *benefits* people? As Christians, we must answer this question within a biblical framework. If the latter is true, it's crucial to establish environmental ethics (and environmental laws) that protect nature independent of human self-interest. These ethics and laws, however, must be in complete harmony with other biblical moral principles.

Although people can and do sin against people, the essential characteristic of all sin is that it's an offense against God (Rom. 8:7; James 4:4). When King David sinned against Uriah and Bathsheba, he understood that ultimately he was sinning against God (see 2 Sam. 11; see also Ps. 51:4). Likewise Joseph recoiled from the sexual advances of Potiphar's wife because to give in to her would "sin against God" (Gen. 39:9). This being the case, exploiting nature would qualify as sin if it too were an offense against God—whether it directly harms people or not.

People were created in God's image and are more valuable to God than plants and animals or rivers and mountains. It is also true, as clearly shown in part two, that creation is important to God *independent* of humanity. God created, loves, and values nature, thereby imputing worth to the land, its wild denizens, and the majesty and beauty of creation—all of which are visible testimonies to God's glory and power (Ps. 19:1; Rom. 1:20). In order to protect nature from abuse and exploitation, God instructed the human race to be His stewards over nature—to oversee and care for His creation and to manage it wisely as God's property.

The fact that God gave the human race stewardship responsibilities over nature implies a moral obligation to God, the moral Lawgiver. God commanded that the human race care for the earth and its creatures. We are to do this both proactively and preemptively. Bouma-Prediger put it well: "It is not enough merely to refrain from doing harm; in certain cases we are morally required to do good. We are obligated to act, not just obligated not to act. Thus, failure to promote the good makes one morally blameworthy."[2] In other words, refusal to obey God's charge to be His stewards over nature would be disobedience and therefore rebellion against God.

Unfortunately, mankind (individually and corporately in their societies) chose to ignore God's stewardship instructions and exploited nature with little regard for its welfare. Disobeying God in any way is sin or lawlessness (1 John 3:4). Thus, environmental exploitation can be considered a sin against God. This can be stated as a syllogism:

Major premise: Disobeying God is sin.
Minor Premise: Environmental exploitation is disobeying God's stewardship mandate.
Conclusion: Therefore, environmental exploitation is a sin against God.

So selfishly exploiting nature *is* sin. The good news is that God never identifies sinful behavior without providing the remedy and a chance for redemption. In terms of destructive environmental exploitation, confession, repentance, and correcting the harm done are necessary, but this also entails accepting and following Bible-based environmental ethics. Although Scripture does not prescribe explicit environmental ethics, it does provide ethical principles and moral guidelines that can legitimately be expanded to encompass environmental issues. In other words, environmental ethics are an inherent part of the total scope of human ethics. The task at hand is to flesh these ethics out of the Bible.

CHAPTER TWELVE

BIBLE-BASED
ENVIRONMENTAL ETHICS

I live in an unincorporated community in the foothills of San Diego County, California. My street ends a third of a mile from home, but a dirt road continues on, passing into national forest land as it winds its way for ten miles through rugged foothills and steep canyons. The native flora in this area is a complex, pungent smelling, densely growing, ever-green shrub community called collectively "chaparral." It is the habitat of mountain lions, bobcats, coyotes, fox, deer, raccoons, opossums, weasels, rattlesnakes, wild turkeys, hawks, and dozens of other varieties of birds, mammals, and reptiles.

A few years ago, five separate wildfires raged across San Diego County, one of them consuming my "local" wilderness. The firestorms began on Sunday, October 23, 2007. Fueled by seventy-plus mph gusts of Santa Ana winds, they burned out of control for days. Across the county, more than 600,000 people (my wife and I included) were evacuated from their homes. Altogether, the conflagrations incinerated nearly 350,000 acres and destroyed more than 1,500 homes, fifty of them in my neighborhood. It burned to within twenty feet of my house!

A few weeks after the fire was extinguished, I rode my mountain bike for several miles along the dirt road. Not a single piece of greenery survived; no wildlife was visible. Only charcoal skeletons of chaparral and, in the canyon bottoms, scorched live oaks and sycamores were all that remained of the pristine "elfin forest."

In spite of the widespread and total devastation, however, the chaparral ecosystem would return to normal in a few years. In His wisdom and love for His creation, God designed nature in such a fashion that a *remnant* of plant and animal life always survives to re-inhabit the land—even after the worst natural disasters. Plants will soon reemerge from sucker roots and dormant seeds. Wildflowers and green grass will burst forth after winter rains. Mammals and reptiles will slowly return. Birds will sing again.

On the day of my bike ride, however, the only signs of "life" in the blackened scrub forest were human: discarded appliances, glass beer bottles, tin cans, and other debris exposed after the fire burned away the brush. As I pondered the irony of this, it occurred to me that what I observed was a picture of humanity's negative impact on nature. While nature will mend itself, if left alone—because God created it that way— human environmental exploitation is much harder to heal.

The illegally discarded human rubbish also reminded me of something else. Today's environmental crisis, at its root, is a moral crisis. The same indifferent and apathetic attitude that compels people to dump rubbish illegally on national forest land likewise prompts the factory owner to dump toxic waste into rivers, pollute the atmosphere with poisonous gases, and destroy vulnerable habitats for economic expediency. It seems to me that only a shift in moral values will tame humanity's intrinsic exploitive behavior and inspire the human race to obey God's charge to be His caretakers over creation.

What is the source and substance of these moral values? Holy Scripture.

The Book of Ethics

The Bible is God's primary channel of revelation to the human race. Paul writes that "All Scripture is God-breathed [inspired] and is useful for teaching, rebuking, correcting and training in righteousness, so that the man of God may be thoroughly equipped for every good work" (2 Tim. 3:16–17). The Bible's moral standards and ethical principles are objective, absolute, obligatory, and applicable to all people and every culture. They are the measurements by which the family of man can judge what is virtuous and condemn evil and immoral behavior. In view of the fact that God instructed the human race to be His caretakers over creation, we can be sure that the Bible contains principles for developing environmental ethics that transcend cultures, societies, religions, and personal and economic self-interest.

By the way, this *isn't* reading environmental ethics back into the Bible. As we saw in chapter 1, because of the limited technology and relatively small human populations in the early centuries of the church, it's understandable that during its formative years the church didn't see the need to identify and develop Bible-based environmental ethics. Be that as it may, searching Scriptures today for spiritual guidance and moral counseling in environmental ethics and stewardship is a legitimate vocation and one that is taking place among many religious traditions, all of whom have historically neglected environmental stewardship.

Old Testament Roots

Old Testament moral law is the foundation on which New Testament ethics rest. Generally, the moral principles referenced in the New Testament are confirmations and restatements of ethical teachings in the Old Testament. Now, this needs some clarification because, as Christians know, many Old Testament laws were set aside under the new covenant initiated by Jesus Christ (Luke 22:20; see also Heb. 7:22; 8:6–7). So, let's take a moment to examine this.

Jewish law in the Old Testament can be categorized under three broad headings. First, are ceremonial (religious) laws. These included the sacrificial system, various religious festivals, and so on. Second are civil laws. These statutes were established to ensure law and order, justice, and fair punishment in Jewish society. Third are moral laws, the core of which are summarized in the Ten Commandments (Exod. 20:1–17).

Jewish ceremonial and civil laws are no longer applicable today because Jesus' sinless life and sacrificial death met the full requirements of the Old Testament law (Matt. 5:17), ushering in the Church Age and a new covenant relationship with God (see Heb. 8:7; 9:15). How do we know this? For one, because Jesus said so (Luke 22:20). Also because nowhere in the New Testament are Jewish ceremonial and civil laws restated or taught. Moral laws, on the other hand, are restated and applied throughout the New Testament—and were taught by Jesus and the apostles. Prohibitions against murder, adultery, stealing, lying, homosexuality, and so on are part and parcel of New Testament ethics. Moral laws reflect the nature of God. They reveal His character and values and thus are timeless and universal ordinances applicable to all people and cultures throughout history.

Why is it important to demonstrate that Old Testament *moral* laws are still applicable today? For two reasons. First, to establish that the foundational moral principles revealed in the Old Testament remain intact in the New Testament. This includes God's directive to mankind to be His stewards over nature—although this particular command was given through Adam to the *entire* human race prior to Jewish law.

The second reason is that it places the authority, clarification, and application of Old Testament moral law under the new covenant established by Jesus Christ (Matt. 5:17). By fulfilling the requirements of the Old Testament law, in particular by living a sinless life (2 Cor. 5:21; Heb. 4:15; 1 John 3:5), Jesus became the ultimate authority, the final word, on ethical behavior and moral law. Let's examine how this plays out in terms of environmental ethics.

Jesus Christ: The Source and Substance of Ethics

Jesus Christ is God incarnate—God in a genuine human body but still fully God (John 1:1, 14). The Bible teaches that Jesus "is the image of the invisible God" (Col. 1:15) and that "in Christ all the fullness of the Deity lives in bodily form" (Col. 2:9). "The Son is the radiance of God's glory and the exact representation of his being" (Heb. 1:3). As God, Jesus is the source and substance of all ethics, and we can extrapolate His teachings to embrace environmental ethics because we know that God loves nature, cares for it, and gave the human race stewardship responsibilities. I like the way John Wesley put it: "I believe in my heart that faith in Jesus Christ can and will lead us beyond an exclusive concern for the well-being of other human beings to the broader concern for the well-being of the birds in our backyards, the fish in our rivers, and every living creature on the face of the earth."[1]

Three fundamental ethical principles taught by Jesus are core ingredients for Bible-based environmental ethics.

Servanthood

Christians are told numerous times to be like Jesus (Rom. 13:14; Eph. 4:24; Phil. 2:5; Col. 3:10). This would include emulating His attitude toward nature. As Tony Campolo observed, "Stewardship over creation means that we should treat creation with the same loving care as Jesus would if He were in our place."[2] In other words, we should develop an attitude toward nature that would duplicate Jesus'.

How did Jesus relate to nature? Although we are not given much information concerning Jesus' personal encounters with nature, we do have a general picture. We know that Jesus enjoyed and appreciated nature. He spent time in natural surroundings: the desert, mountains, gardens, and the Sea of Galilee. His greatest recorded sermon took place on a mountain (Matt. 5:1). In order to escape the stress and pressure of ministry, Jesus sometimes withdrew to the wilderness to be alone (Matt. 14:12–13; Luke 5:15–16; John 6:15) and encouraged His follows to do likewise (Mark 6:31). (Anyone who has spent time alone in woods or desert can appreciate the restorative power and calming effect that nature must have had on Jesus and His apostles.) Jesus wove many of His parables and teachings around natural settings (Matt. 13:3–9, 24–32; Mark 4:26–29). He admired the lilies of the field and birds of the air and pointed out that God cares for and protects them (Matt. 6:26–29; Luke 12:6, 24). Wild animals accompanied Jesus during His temptation in the wilderness (Mark 1:13). Most convincing is the fact that Jesus and the Father (along with the Holy Spirit) are one in essence in the triune Godhead (John 10:30, 38). It would be impossible theologically for Christ not to love and care for nature the same as the Father does (Job 38, 39; Ps. 104; Matt. 6:26).

Perhaps the most important characteristic of Jesus, in terms of developing a theology of environmental ethics, is that He saw Himself as a servant (Matt. 20:28), and He expected His followers to be servants also (John 13:5–17). Consider the following passage:

> Your attitude should be the same as that of Christ Jesus:
>
> > Who, being in very nature God,
> > > did not consider equality with God something
> > > > to be grasped [i.e., asserted],
> > > but made himself nothing,
> > > taking the very nature of a servant,
> > > being made in human likeness. (Phil. 2:5–7)

This passage instructs believers to have the same attitude as Jesus Christ. The apostle Paul prefaced this passage by warning us, "Do nothing out of selfish ambition or vain conceit, but in humility consider others better than yourselves. Each of you should look not only to your own interests, but also to the interests of others" (vv. 3–4). Jesus came to earth and took on "the very nature of a servant" (v. 7). If we adopt the "attitude" of Christ, we will become servants of *God*.

What does this mean with regard to our stewardship responsibilities over nature? As Savior, Jesus took our sins to the cross and died on our behalf, opening the door to reconciliation with God (Rom. 5:8; 8:1). Does this mean that as servants of God the human race should consider themselves "saviors" of nature in the sense of paving the way for its reconciliation? Some theologians have argued that we should.

In chapter 7, we studied biblical passages that revealed that mankind's redemption would include nature's redemption from the curse (Rom. 8:19–23). Moreover, we learned that the Bible teaches that our redemption begins the moment we enter the family of Christ (when we are born again, John 3:3), and that we are to live and behave as redeemed people in *this* life. As God's stewards over creation, we are to put into practice strategies that will protect nature in the here and now. Thus, it is not a theological stretch to say that just as Jesus loves us and became our Savior, so too should we not only love other people as Christ loves us, but also consider the outflow of our servanthood to include being "saviors" of nature under Christ's direction and authority. Christian environmental ethicist and theologian Loren Wilkinson commented on this:

> Christians place at the center of their faith the example of one who . . . became a servant. The implication is clear: what God became for us, we are to become for nature. . . .
>
> Humans are to become saviors of nature, as Christ is the savior of humanity (and hence, through humans, of nature). . . .
>
> This idea of humans as the saviors of nature is not simply theological speculation. It is implied in all of those many Scripture passages which speak of redeemed humans as "joint-heirs" with Christ. As Christ is Ruler, Creator, and Sustainer of the world, so also is man to be. Being heirs with Christ involves (as Paul saw) being crucified with Christ; it also involves sharing in the sustaining activity of Christ the Creator.[3]

Unconditional Love

In the New Testament, the English word *love* is translated from several Greek words, each with a distinct meaning. For example, the Greek word *philadelphia* describes "brotherly love," Christians' love for each other (e.g., Rom. 12:10). It is not used to describe God's love for people or vice versa. The Greek word used to describe God's love for people is *agape*. It's a love that denotes a willful choice. It's the love that God bestows on people, not because we deserve it, but because He chooses to love us in spite of our sin and rebellion. It's unconditional love. This kind of love is not based on feelings or emotions. *Agape* "involves God doing what is best for man and not necessarily what man desires."[4] Jesus said in John 14:15, "If you love me, you will obey what I command." He didn't say we would obey Him if we feel like it, but we will obey Him if we "love" (*agape*) Him. We choose to obey Jesus even if we don't want to.

If people wish to exhibit the attitude of love that Jesus has, they will show evidence of an *agape* kind of love. They will make choices that are designed to do what is best for the object loved, in spite of desires to do otherwise. This has direct ramifications for environmental ethics. Servanthood, based on the "attitude" of Christ, is motivated out of selfless, unconditional, willful love. It is a natural outflow of God's love for us (see Rom. 5:5; Gal. 5:13). We become caretakers of nature not just because we are instructed to do so by virtue of our stewardship responsibilities, but also because we love God. Furthermore, we will make ecological and environmental decisions that may not always be in our best interest (i.e., political and economic gain) if they are in the best interest of nature, such as setting aside wetlands for wildlife habitats and protecting endangered or threatened predators (such as wolves) that may prey on the game animals that hunters like to kill. As "saviors" of nature, we will make choices that will advance our redemptive role as nature's protector and steward.

The Golden Rule

Loren Wilkinson pointed out, "It is just as possible to misuse dominion toward nature as it is to misuse it toward humans. And if the pattern for our use of power is established in Christ, then it is a pattern for our treatment of nature, as well as of humanity."[5] The pattern for our treatment of humanity was clearly set forth by Jesus in a beloved passage Christians call the Golden Rule: "So in everything, do to others what you would have them do to you, for this sums up the Law and the Prophets" (Matt. 7:12). This life-changing "rule"—grounded in *agape*—extends even to the point of forfeiting one's life for a friend (John 15:13). At the very least, Christians are expected to "forgo one's comfort and material security— for the sake of another."[6]

Although this rule is directed to people's relationships with people, the principle behind the Golden Rule could logically and theologically be inclusive to all life God created and values. People will not be called upon to sacrifice their lives or well being for the benefit of a plant or animal, but the mind-set of treating nature in the same fashion we want nature to treat us would benefit humanity and nature alike.

Nature provides numerous services free of charge. It manufactures oxygen, filters our water, cleans our air, and provides nutrients for soil—not to mention its aesthetic and spiritual benefits. Virtually every vitamin and mineral nutrient needed by the human body (and many useful medicines and balms that bring healing and relief from suffering) are derived from plants. If the human race wants to continue reaping the incalculable benefits nature provides—which we usually take for granted or are not even aware of—we must watch over it, protect it, and use its resources with wise stewardship. This means not polluting our environment, not destroying wildlife habitats, and not exterminating plant and animal species.

The Balance

To sum up, the biblical view of environmental ethics balances human material needs with moral obligations to ensure the welfare of God's creation. Developing environmental ethics is no more complicated than extending traditional Christian ethics to the natural realm. Religious writers Denise and John Carmody summarized it well:

> To make friends of the earth, Christianity would have us whittle away the vices that incline us to abuse the earth. These are largely the same vices that incline us to abuse our fellow human beings and thwart social justice: love of riches, love of honors, and pride. . . . Those who concentrate on riches, honors, or their own great worth lose their balance and slip into vice. Vice is precisely imbalance, missing the golden mean. Regarding nature, it shows in the very destructive effects of

today's industrialization. . . . All over the developed world, we have let greed blind us to a great poisoning of the environment.[7]

Jesus warned us in Luke 12:15 to "be on your guard against all kinds of greed; a man's life does not consist in the abundance of his possessions." If the human sins of greed, covetousness, and pride were eliminated from our relationship with nature, as we are told in Scripture to eliminate them from our relationship with people, we would operate our factories and develop our natural resources for profit—but not at the expense of destructive environmental exploitation and consequent degradation. We would seek renewable sources of energy and develop more efficient and energy-saving cars and machines; factories would implement safeguards against air and water pollution; people would conscientiously recycle metals, plastics, and wood products; wildlife habitats would be protected; abandoned strip mines would be restored to natural habitats. As Francis Schaeffer insisted, the human race "must voluntarily limit [itself]. . . . We must not allow ourselves individually, [nor] our technology, to do everything we or it can do."[8]

The cardinal ethical principles of servanthood, unconditional love, and the Golden Rule can effectively guide our stewardship activities over nature and promote an attitude toward the land that ensures the welfare of both humanity and nature. No other religion or humanist philosophy contains so precise and explicit ethical principles as the Bible. As long as people make stewardship decisions within its ethical guidelines, thereby caring for the whole household of creation, we will be fulfilling our responsibility as God's ordained stewards over nature.

We are nearing the end of our study. It's time to turn our attention to hands-on practical matters. What, specifically, can the church—corporately and locally—do to implement strategies and programs that will fulfill our responsibilities as God's ordained caretakers of nature? This is the subject of the next chapter.

CHAPTER THIRTEEN

THE CHURCH IN ACTION

n June 1974, a few years after the first Earth Day (April 22, 1970), I published my first "I actually got paid for it!" magazine article. It was titled "Helping Children Learn an Ecology Value." Drawing from experiences with my family, I suggested ways that parents could instill in their youngsters an appreciation of nature and moral values to govern their behavior regarding the land and its wild denizens. My strategy was to take kids outdoors and show them how amazing nature is and why it's worth protecting.

I pulled the article out of my personal archives a while back and reread it. I confess it grieved me. When I look at the world today, it's clear that most people have yet to embrace an "ecology value" that vigorously promotes stewardship. Many of the ecological and environmental problems that existed nearly forty years ago still exist. And, as we saw in chapter 1, with video games, the Internet, and many dozens of TV stations to entertain them, not only children but adults spend far less time outdoors experiencing the sights, sounds, and smells of nature today than they did in the 1970s.

I see my attempt to instill an ecology value in children as analogous to what the church must do in modern society. Jesus and the apostles instructed believers to lead by example (see Matt. 5:16; 1 Peter 2:12). With regard to environmental ethics and stewardship, if a pro-environmental transformation occurs within the Christian community, the church will be in a position to take a leadership role in implementing values and strategies that will foster real changes in environment-related activities. With this in mind, the purpose of this chapter is to suggest ways in which the church can lead by example. Then, in the following chapter, we'll explore the impact this can have on Christian evangelism and worldwide missions.

Religious Reformation

Throughout human history, ethical principles and moral behavior have always been grounded in religious beliefs. Consequently, solutions to the environmental crisis will require religious reformation as much as technological innovation. Indeed, since technology running amok is the instrument of destructive environmental exploitation, technology itself must operate under the supervision of ethical guidelines.

In the godless world of naturalistic evolution, Homo sapiens are the pinnacles of an evolutionary hierarchy. Survival of the fittest carried to its logical and philosophical conclusion, demands that nature be submissive to human needs, wants, and desires. There is no ethical basis to establish, validate, or defend moral values (including environmental ethics and stewardship) that are counterproductive to human self-interest. To be consistent, an evolutionary paradigm requires that the earth and its wild creatures have only instrumental value according to what humans assign to them. Ironically, it's not the biblical worldview that would promote environmental exploitation and abuse. It's the ideology of godless naturalistic evolution, played out in human greed and consumption, which allows people to freely use and abuse nature for purely selfish gain.[1]

The Christian worldview, on the other hand, has an objective and transcendent basis for establishing environmental ethics: God. Nature matters to God. He created it (Gen. 1:1). He provides water, food, and habitats for wildlife (Ps. 104). He takes pleasure in nature (Pss. 50:10–11; 104:31). It has God-given intrinsic value independent of human self-interest—and thus God instructed the human race to care for and to protect the land and its wild inhabitants.

When we consider the scale of environmental degradation worldwide, it can seem like an impossible task to halt, let alone correct, the damage being done to the earth. Yet Christians must keep in mind that environmental stewardship is obeying God. Our job is to be faithful to that commission. We must accept our responsibilities, but it is God's job to change the hearts of people and nations so that they recognize the damage being done to the earth; to convict them of the danger that continued destructive environmental exploitation will have, not only to nature, but also to the entire human race; and then to prompt people and nations to take the steps necessary to heal our natural environments, protect the earth's remaining wild lands and its free-living inhabitants, clean up air and water pollution, and carefully manage our natural resources in a sustainable fashion. In short, we are to do God's work in a Christ-honoring way; it's up to Him to ensure that it bears fruit. And this can happen because, as Professor John Houghton put it, our "partner is none other than God himself."[2]

The role of the church in developing and putting into practice pro-environmental strategies can be examined on three levels: the church as a single entity (the universal church), a community of believers (the local church), and individual members of the body of Christ (1 Cor. 12:27). Each has a role to play in institutionalizing environmental ethics and activities.

The Universal Church

The environmental crisis is a worldwide one. Deforestation, desertification, extermination of plants and animals, and water and air pollution affect all nations and people. Historically, the church corporately has failed to respond to this crisis. In fact, it has sometimes twisted and perverted biblical texts to justify misusing and exploiting nature. As much as anyone else, Christians have degraded God's creative work and harbored attitudes that devalue nature as merely something to be used for human consumption.

The first step to developing Bible-based environmental ethics and formulating a strategy of environmental stewardship is for the church corporately to admit its failure to obey God's stewardship instructions. As with any sin, the church must confess its destructive behavior through prayer and repent of attitudes and activities that devalue God's creation. Once repentant and united in purpose, the church should seek to identify, affirm, and disseminate biblical principles and moral values that foster environmental stewardship.

As demonstrated in chapter 3, no religion is better equipped theologically and morally than Christianity to confront today's environmental and ecological crisis. Theologian Frederick Elder spoke to this in his book, *Crisis in Eden: A Religious Study of Man and Environment*:

> With the sovereign God the churches have in their possession the one reference that can meaningfully shift attention away from man. Understanding God as far more than the deity whose only concern is man, the churches, better than other institutions, can have good reason to insist that man must turn in a new direction if he is to avoid disaster. . . .
>
> The churches could emerge from their ethical parochialism and, armed with empirical and aesthetic, as well as biblical and theological data, could lead the country, and through it the entire planet, back from the brink of ecological disaster on which it presently teeters. This would be a world-saving endeavor, but that, in one form or another, has always been the mission of the Savior's Church.[3]

Elder understood that the Christian church not only has the responsibility and authority to initiate environmental ethics, it has the *capability*. The church draws huge numbers of people every Sunday. In the United States, 70 percent of evangelicals (and 46 percent of the total United States population) attend church at least once a week.[4] Worldwide, Christians encompass approximately one-third of the earth's population. Thus, the audience to which Christian environmental ethics can be promulgated is enormous. If the church in America accepts its stewardship responsibilities over creation as set forth in the Bible and *puts them into practice*, their numbers could conceivably bring about the momentum needed to institutionalize environmental ethics across the United States and ultimately the entire planet. Success will depend largely upon the actions, unity of purpose, and commitments of the entire Christian church.

A paradigm shift in the church's historic relationship with nature—a regeneration of attitudes and actions—can have a powerful evangelistic dimension throughout the entire church and its many ministries. In popular culture, more often than not, the Christian church is perceived as indifferent to environmental matters and opposed to environmental activism; we don't want the gospel rejected for that reason. If the church corporately takes a leadership role in becoming a public voice *against* environmental exploitation and actively promotes environmental stewardship and conservation, it will demonstrate that Christians do care about nature and the environment. This will attract many people who may have previously been uninterested in Christianity. In particular, Bible-based environmentalism can be an evangelistic outreach to American environmentalists and nature lovers who left the church—at least in part—because of its pervasive dismissal of environmental and ecological stewardship. This is especially true of young people (in particular, college students) who, overall, are more sensitive to environmental concerns than the American population at large. We'll look more closely at the evangelistic opportunities embedded in Christian environmentalism in the following chapter.

The Local Church

During the past decade, millions of Christians have become more environmentally conscious. According to a study by the Barna Group, 78 percent of "self-identified" Christians "would like to see their fellow Christians take a more active role in caring for God's creation in a way that is both informed and biblical."[5] More evidence of this is a National Association of Evangelicals (NAE) document titled "For the Health of the

Nation: An Evangelical Call to Civic Responsibility." (The NAE represents 45,000 local churches in more than forty different denominations.) The document includes the statement:

> As we embrace our responsibility to care for God's earth, we reaffirm the important truth that we worship only the Creator and not the creation. God gave the care of his earth and its species to our first parents. That responsibility has passed into our hands. We affirm that God-given dominion is a sacred responsibility to steward the earth and not a license to abuse the creation of which we are a part. We are not the owners of creation, but its stewards, summoned by God to "watch over and care for it" (Gen. 2:15). This implies the principle of sustainability: our uses of the Earth must be designed to conserve and renew the Earth rather than to deplete or destroy it.[6]

Equally significant are movements on Christian college campuses that stress environmental activism. An article in *Christianity Today* reported, "Integrating creation care with academics is a growing emphasis on Christian campuses around the country. According to Paul Corts, president of the interdenominational Council for Christian Colleges and Universities (CCCU), about 40 of 105 North American member schools have adopted significant green initiatives."[7]

Local churches are also being encouraged to participate in practical—and money saving—stewardship activities. A speaker at an NAE luncheon observed:

> "If America's more than 300,000 houses of worship cut energy use by 10 percent, they would save nearly $200 million each year—money that could be used for missions and other priorities," says Richard Cizik, Vice President of Governmental Affairs for the NAE. "It would also prevent the annual release

of more than 2 million tons of greenhouse gas emissions, which is equivalent to the emissions generated by about 400,000 cars or the planting of over a half million acres of trees."[8]

Christians are told to lead by example. Good "eco-friendly" policies ought to be an essential part of the local church. Maintenance programs should include periodic energy audits to ensure the most efficient use of electricity and gas. Cleaning supplies should be biodegradable or "green". All churches can initiate recycling programs and encourage the use of ceramic mugs, glasses, and plates instead of Styrofoam and cardboard. Landscaping with native plants (especially in the Southwest) will conserve water and fertilizers. Many churches have undeveloped land, which can be used as community gardens (also a good outreach to the neighborhood). Building programs should consider architectural designs that require less energy to heat and cool. In some areas, solar or wind power can virtually eliminate or greatly reduce energy costs.

The emerging ecological consciousness within Christendom has spawned a number of faith-based environmental organizations, such as Evangelical Environmental Network and the Au Sable Institute of Environmental Studies. These parachurch ministries are widely respected centers for Bible-based environmental education, training, and mobilization. They support a sensible, balanced environmentalism that acknowledges humanity's rightful place in the world's ecosystems. They encourage and support policies that allow mankind to use natural resources for shelter, nourishment, and technology—yet in a fashion that does not damage the land, pollute the air, poison water, or threaten the extinction of other life forms. Christian environmental ministries also seek to raise people's appreciation of the beauty and magnificence of creation and the value of its incredibly diverse inhabitants—both plant and animal.

Important as these parachurch ministries are, however, it is still the local church that must take the initiative to teach environmental ethics and stewardship.

The work of Christ here on earth is carried out primarily by individual Christians serving together through the ministries of local churches. Thus, it falls on the shoulders of churches to broadcast and live out the biblical message of environmental stewardship and to carry Christ-centered environmental ethics into the non-Christian world. In order to do this, education is crucial. Dr. Mary H. Korte, director of the Environmental Education Program at Concordia University, Wisconsin, had it right when she wrote: "Because many environmental problems must be remedied and avoided in the future, instruction in environmental science and environmental ethics should be included in the curriculum of Christian schools from prekindergarten through post-secondary institutions. All students should be taught not only *how* but also *why* Christians are called to practice wise environmental stewardship of nature."[9]

Teaching environmental ethics and stewardship in local churches and Christian schools can be accomplished in a variety of ways. It's crucial, however, that pastors take the leadership role *from the pulpit.* Sermons could include a systematic study of the biblical environmental doctrine developed in chapters 5 through 9—as well as the moral principles Jesus taught that apply directly to environmental ethics (chapter 12). This teaching should trickle down to adult and youth Sunday school classes, home fellowships, and even church discipleship programs. In sum, local churches should embark on an enthusiastic teaching and training program to educate their body on the biblical perspective of environmental stewardship.

Many resources are available for this. Parachurch environmental ministries offer lectures, classes, and materials for adult Sunday school, youth ministries, and small group studies. Resources are also available to help mobilize eco-friendly projects, such as tree planting, recycling programs, and trash cleanup. Church sponsored seminars on environmental stewardship that are open to the community can be an effective outreach ministry. Pastor and author Tri Robinson wrote a book on his church's experiences developing an environmental stewardship ministry.[10] It includes a list of environmental organizations, ministries, and resources that are available on his website (www.savinggodsgreenearth.com). Professor of environmental studies Calvin DeWitt, in his book *Earth-Wise*, provides a comprehensive plan for developing "Creation Care Centers" in local churches.[11]

Another way to raise people's awareness of environmental concerns—as well as a greater appreciation of nature—is to promote church-sponsored outdoor recreational activities such as camping, day hiking, backpacking, and bird and wildlife watching.[12] This can be combined with conservation activities, such as trail maintenance, cleaning up trash, removing noxious weeds, and similar outdoor programs (always under the supervision of the appropriate officials). These "hands-on" activities can be especially enlightening to young people, who often spend an inordinate amount of time indoors and may never have experienced nature firsthand. Pastor Tri Robinson made an important observation relevant to this.

> Stewardship is a value to be passed from generation to generation, emphasizing the great importance of caring for God's creation. Most of the values we adopt from our parents are "caught," actions and behavior we observe and absorb. What our parents *say* to us is important, but what they *do* leaves an indelible mark on who we are as we grow up and mature. . . .
>
> Organized camping trips, where many parents took their children into the woods with other families for wilderness cleanup and restoration projects . . . [allowed kids to see] firsthand ecological values being lived out by their parents. When we model how to steward what God has given us, our children will catch the lifestyle and it will become part of who they are."[13]

The point of all these activities is to elevate the ecological consciousness of the church family and to encourage the local body to model behaviors that reflect responsible environmental stewardship.

The Individual Christian

Jesus exhorted His followers, "Let your light shine before men, that they may see your good deeds and praise your Father in heaven" (Matt. 5:16). The apostle Peter reiterated: "Live such good lives among the pagans [i.e., unbelievers] that, though they accuse you of doing wrong, they may see your good deeds and glorify God on the day he visits us" (1 Peter 2:12). In terms of Bible-based environmentalism, this can play out in two ways.

Practical Application

Individual Christians can do many things that will contribute solutions to environmental degradation. We can support public policies that promote sensible approaches to environmental stewardship and conservation. We can write editorials in local newspapers and e-mail letters to elected officials stating our desire for them to promote recycling programs and energy conservation, protect endangered and threatened wildlife, and set aside land for native plants and animals. Since many environmental issues are local, we can volunteer to serve on planning boards, participate in local environmental surveys, and attend zoning hearings that will affect population growth and commercial development.

In the late 1970s, the city of San Diego was negotiating with a large developer to set aside one of the city's few remaining coastal canyons as a natural park. Since I had explored the six-mile-long canyon, in order to garner public support, I wrote an article for a small local newspaper that described the various habitats in the canyon and the wildlife living there. It was a small thing, but when I visit the canyon today I'm proud that I was part of the movement to set aside this beautiful natural park.

All Christians can recycle aluminum and other metals, glass, plastic, and newspapers. (A good resource for information on recycling is www .eco-cycle.org.) Americans throw away an estimated 380 billion plastic bags or wraps every year.[14] Many of these bags (and other synthetic materials) end up in marine environments, where fish, dolphins, whales, seals, and birds get entangled in them or mistake the debris for food. A United Nations study in 2006 estimated that there are 46,000 floating pieces of plastic *per square mile* of ocean.[15] Instead of using plastic or paper grocery bags, we can purchase cloth for around a dollar in many grocery stores. We can insulate and weather-strip our homes (energy companies will sometimes subsidize these projects), turn down thermostats, conserve water, and when possible drive more energy-efficient cars. In a word, following Jesus' teaching that life does not consist of an abundance of possessions (Luke 12:15), we can live simpler lives by being prudent and exercising restraint, thereby curtailing excessive and unnecessary consumption. Such a lifestyle testifies to non-Christians that Christians are not apathetic to ecological problems. Perhaps more important, it demonstrates that Christian environmental ethics can result in real conservation and stewardship practices.

Professor Bouma-Prediger adds an encouraging note with regard to living a simpler, less consumer-focused lifestyle:

> Cultural norms to the contrary, more is not necessarily better, for us or for the earth. As social psychologist David Myers [of Hope College] concludes after an exhaustive review of the literature, there is no correlation whatsoever between wealth and well-being. He goes on to affirm, "Realizing that well-being is something other than being well-off is liberating." A simpler way of life liberates us from emulating "the lifestyle of the rich and famous" and thereby enables us to find authentic happiness. . . . In sum, we should care for the earth because an earth-friendly way of life is simply more joyful.[16]

Spiritual Application

Environmentalism is not a religion. Nor is the earth the center of our existence. That would smack of neo-paganism. Jesus Christ is the center of our existence and the earth and all things "live and move and have [their] being" in Him (Acts 17:28). Christian environmentalism is always "theocentric," that is, we care for nature but we serve and worship God.

Having said this, there is a spiritual dimension to Christian environmentalism. If we love God, we should love what He loves. God loves and cares for His creation. Therefore, followers of Jesus Christ should seek to develop a respectful reverence for God's creation.

This can begin during our personal devotions. Time should be dedicated to reflection and prayer on what God would have us to do as His caretakers over creation. It may be necessary to confess and repent for ways in which we have personally damaged God's creative work (perhaps unknowingly) or neglected, out of laziness or indifference, to take simple steps to care for it—such as the modest activity of recycling. We can pray for the survival and protection of endangered species of animals and for greater environmental sensitivity among those who dishonor God by abusing and despoiling creation. We can pray that our elected officials will show greater concern for environmental issues. We can pray for opportunities to share the gospel with non-Christian environmentalists and nature lovers by explaining—as an apologetic point of contact—that Jesus' work of reconciliation includes the redemption of nature as well as believers (see chapter 7).

The apologetic and evangelistic opportunities available through sound biblical environmentalism lead us to our final chapter.

CHAPTER FOURTEEN

ECOLOGICAL EVANGELISM

Every Thursday at 6 AM I meet with eight other Christian men for an hour and a half book discussion. I wrote an article on Christian environmentalism for the September/October 2010 issue of the *Christian Research Journal*,[1] and shortly after it was published gave copies to the group so we could discuss it the following week. Since environmentalism is a controversial topic among Christians, I was curious to hear their comments.

I was not surprised to discover that none of the men had ever considered the theological implications of environmentalism, or their responsibilities before God to be good stewards over the earth. But I was pleasantly surprised that none of the men had a problem with acknowledging this responsibility. We even talked about ways our church could become more ecologically efficient.

This topic, however, turned out to be only a small part of our discussion. Very quickly it shifted to the climate change controversy and the widespread assumption among Christians that most environmentalists are left-leaning extremists whose real motives are political power and government funding. Global warming, they believe, is a prime example. It's greatly exaggerated to further environmentalists' political and economic schemes.

The suspicion that deception and hidden agendas prompt environmentalists to forecast ecological doomsday scenarios is a huge stumbling block for many Christians, and a major reason they are reluctant to endorse environmentalism. Global warming in particular has become such a polarizing political hot potato that it often short-circuits potential dialogue between Christians and environmentalists even before it can begin.

This is exactly what happened in my discussion group. I had to get the group beyond the global warming controversy before we could discuss biblical environmental stewardship. Since this is a stumbling block for many Christians—and thus an obstacle to evangelizing non-Christian environmentalists—I want to share how I dealt with it.

I pointed out that the controversy over climate change should not distract us from our moral obligation to be obedient to God's stewardship mandate. The cause of climate change is a debatable issue that has yet to be fully determined. In the meantime, we are obliged to keep our focus on being faithful stewards of God's creation. If we do that, we'll make right choices if it turns out global warming *is* human caused and damaging God's green earth. In short, I handled this issue with my Christian friends by defusing it.

I'm sharing this anecdote as a prelude to the rest of this chapter. There is great evangelistic potential in Christian environmentalism, and we can't forfeit these opportunities because of our own biases and misconceptions. Good evangelism does not create obstacles; it removes them. If our perspective is in sync with Scripture, we can use Christian environmentalism as an effective door to evangelism.

Ecological Apologetics

When it comes to sharing the gospel with non-Christians—environmentalists or otherwise—apologetics is often a necessary ingredient in evangelism. Apologetics is a study in the defense of Christianity. It marshals rational, objective, testable evidences that demonstrate Christian truth claims are true. The Bible is historically reliable. Jesus is who He claims to be: fully God and fully man. The resurrection is a fact of history. Creation occurred by divine decree. And so on. This entire book is essentially an apologetics for Christian environmentalism. It defends a well-defined biblical doctrine of environmental ethics and stewardship and refutes secular and religious claims that challenge it.

In today's secular and postmodern world, many non-Christians are ignorant of what the Bible teaches and often form their opinions about Christianity (and Christians) from popular culture: academia, the media, and the entertainment industries. This includes the prevailing view among many environmentalists that the Bible allows people to use and abuse nature without regard to the consequences to nature and its wild inhabitants. Here's where apologetics can come into play.

The purpose of apologetics is to identify and remove obstacles that prevent non-Christians from accepting Christ, and recognizing Christianity as a valid world-and-life view. In the case of non-Christian environmentalists, their mistaken belief that the Bible justifies ecological abuse and harmful exploitation can be that obstacle. The apologetic challenge, then, is how to explain to non-Christian environmentalists the true biblical teachings on environmental ethics and stewardship, and to do so in a way that gets a fair hearing.

Points of Contact

In my book *Engaging the Closed Minded*, I explain how to initiate a "point of contact" when discussing topics that concern both Christians and non-Christians but on which there is disagreement.[2] A point of contact is an area of *mutual* agreement. It is a starting point from which productive dialogue can blossom and lead to the Christian perspective on the issue at hand. Let me illustrate this.

When my wife and I were active in the Sierra Club in the late 1970s and early 1980s, we went on several club-sponsored backpacks. On one such trip, I stopped to rest with a fellow "clubber" at an elevated spot overlooking a beautiful desert valley. I can still visualize him looking across a panorama that would qualify for a calendar photograph. As he gazed about, he made a comment like this: "This is my church. This is where you can feel close to God!"

I was not a Christian at the time (and neither was he), but for purposes of this illustration I will pretend I was, and I'll also assume that this person believed most Christians couldn't care less about environmental stewardship. Had this been the case, I would have responded like this:

"I agree. You can feel close to God out here in the wilderness." (This part of our conversation was true, and I did and do agree with him.) "But since you mention it, I'd like to ask you something. If God created all this beauty, do you suppose He *wants* us to feel His presence out here?" After giving him a chance to respond, I would follow up with a statement like this: "There are verses in the Bible that confirm what you are feeling is real. People can feel close to God in nature. But there's more to it than that. I believe another reason God reveals His presence in creation is because He wants people to take responsibility to care for it. I know you think most Christians couldn't care less about what happens to nature, and in some cases I admit that's true. But then so do a lot of non-Christians. But the fact is, God is an environmentalist too! The Bible teaches this. What do you think about that?"

Do you see how I would have used this encounter as an apologetic point of contact? I agreed that people can feel close to God in nature. The Bible confirms it. My hiking pal's feelings were real. I even acknowledged that some Christians are apathetic to environmental concerns. These comments would have established a point of common ground—an area of mutual agreement—from which positive dialogue could begin. I then moved the conversation to the Christian perspective, one he likely had never heard. I suggested that the Bible teaches that God wants all people to be His caretakers over creation. To drive this claim home, I made a provocative statement that God is an environmentalist.

Eventually, I would have attempted to move the conversation from apologetics to evangelism (the goal of all apologetics) by asking a relevant transitional question such as, "Did you know Jesus sought time alone in nature to rest and pray? Apparently He felt close to God the Father in the wilderness, too."

Even if our conversation did not lead to a gospel presentation, at the least I would have demonstrated that biblical Christianity is not apathetic to ecological and environmental problems. God is very concerned about the welfare of creation and instructed the human race to be His caretakers. If my hiking companion accepted this, I would have done my job as ecological apologist.

Targeting Youth

Statistically, most people who become Christians do so between childhood and college. When young people leave home and begin living independently, they are more likely to adopt the world's values and viewpoints and less likely to become Christians. Sadly, this is also true of professing Christians. Up to 80 percent of young people raised in *Christian* homes walk away from their faith during their college years.[3]

I believe Christian environmental activism could play a pivotal role in curtailing this trend as well as attracting non-Christian young people to the faith. Demographically, young people today are more likely to be unchurched than in past generations. Thus, ecological evangelism can be particularly effective with non-Christian high school and college age people.

Stephen Rand of the Evangelical Alliance Relief Fund (Tearfund) writes: "The enthusiasm of the young people [for God's calling to care for creation] was encouraging, but not surprising: every survey showed that the environment was top of the list of their concerns for the future."[4] The church, however, must capitalize on this. Rand continues:

> What quickly became clear was that, while these young people were deeply concerned about the environment, they had never heard anything about it in their churches. . . .
>
> The church is called to a holistic witness that includes both the proclamation and demonstration of the good news that offers eternal life, life in all its fullness. Yet in failing to teach young people the relevant biblical truths that could build a truly Christian approach to the environment, the church has

been closing the door on a vital route for the gospel. Its silence was—and is—a tragic missed opportunity of culturally relevant evangelism.[5]

Lifestyle Evangelism

When non-Christian environmentalists—young or old—observe Christians sincerely showing concern for the natural environment and its wild denizens, when they observe Christians engaged in eco-friendly activities, it can create major evangelistic opportunities. Edward R. Brown, founding director of the environmental mission agency Care of Creation, explains:

> Letting our friends and neighbors see us as people who love and care for God's world can give us a powerful bridge to relationships. Sharing such a fundamental value can—and often does—become a platform for sharing many other things, including our love for Jesus and our desire that others would learn to love him too. . . .
>
> There is no question that a vigorous and visible creation-care program will go a long way toward enhancing and enriching any evangelistic outreach program [the church] already [has], just as it will enrich worship and improve children's programs.[6]

Ecological lifestyle evangelism should include inviting non-Christian friends—and the community at large—to join us in creation care activities (see chapter 13). When they work side-by-side with Christians on ecological projects, we have opportunities to befriend them and to invite them to visit our churches.

Author and pastor Tri Robinson, who includes ecological programs as part of his church ministry, comments on this:

> Through becoming faithful stewards of creation, we are presented with an opportunity to share the Gospel. In becoming

leaders in this area, we won't be selling out to a culturally compromised gospel; rather, we will be faithful in contextualizing
the Gospel in our own nation as well as making it real for
other people groups around the world. . . .

Many people are often enamored with the beauty of the
world around them, yet they haven't yet met the Creator. . . .
Environmental ministry outreach not only puts believers in
the community but it puts them working hand in hand with
those who have not yet received Christ. In outreach, making
the connection and building relationships is 90 percent of the
work—and usually the hardest. Eventually, when other people
begin to see the light of Jesus alive in us, the opportunities to
share our faith will come . . . and they come at their request.[7]

Christian Missions

This same evangelistic outreach can play out on a worldwide scale. As
Edward Brown further points out, "Healing creation is one of the most
meaningful, practical and long-lasting ways we can love our neighbors.
This is probably most obvious when we think of missions and the way in
which people in developing countries are suffering from the effects of environmental degradation."[8]

Millions of people die every year for lack of a healthy, sustainable environment, and many millions more are forced to leave their homes due
to a variety of environmental disasters. According to the World Health
Association, some of the leading causes of death in developing countries
are poor nutrition, contaminated water, and poor sanitary conditions.
Environmental degradation almost always results in poverty and disease.
Nature is not the only thing that suffers when natural environments dete-
riorate. The poor also suffer.

It's understandable that poverty and hunger force people to misuse
their environments. It's not that poor people *want* to degrade their environments; it's a matter of feeding their families in order to survive.
The poor in undeveloped countries have no ability to reverse this trend.

They must continue to deplete their environments just to meet their basic needs—creating a devastating downward spiral into ever more environmental degradation and consequent poverty. As the Christian creation care document *An Evangelical Declaration on the Care of Creation* puts it, "Human poverty is both the cause and a consequence of environmental degradation."[9] Christians can help remedy this through practical ecological aid.

Just as missionary organizations send doctors, teachers, and builders into impoverished countries, the church can open the door to the gospel by sending ecologists, conservationists, and other environmental specialists who can teach people proper sanitation techniques and how to get the most out of cultivation by adhering to fundamental ecological principles. Missionary-minded environmentalism, which should include programs such as drilling wells to reach clean drinking water and training farmers to use their land without destroying or contaminating it, could help eliminate malnutrition and many communicable diseases. Certainly the goal of such aid is not just to share the gospel. It's to help impoverished people live healthier, longer lives and to raise their standard of living. Nevertheless, imagine the evangelistic opportunities available if an emphasis on environmental stewardship were added to our missionary outreach. Teaching people to care for their environment is an extension of caring for people themselves, which all Christians are called to do (see Matt. 25:40; John 3:17; James 2:15–16).

So, Should Christians Be Environmentalists?

Today's environmental crisis is not a fabrication of the liberal left, as some pundits would have us believe. Vast portions of the earth have been gravely damaged by human exploitation, and it's getting worse every year. It is crucial that the present generation develop ethical guidelines based on a biblical environmental doctrine to govern modern technology, industry, and recreational activities. The consequences of failing to do this could be catastrophic on a worldwide scale. On the other hand, it will be a great honor to God—an attitude of worship, obedience, and commit-ment—if the human race accepts its responsibility to protect, care for, and enjoy God's marvelous creation.

I want to close this chapter with a beautifully worded "Christian Land Ethic Statement" from the Au Sable Institute of Environmental Studies. It summarizes perfectly the source and substance of Christian environmental stewardship. Why should Christians be environmentalists? Here's why:

> Ultimately, all life belongs to God, who sustains us in and through the land. Consequently, the destiny of the land and humanity are inextricably intertwined and must be recognized in thought and action. The creation is no commodity to be bought and sold, used and abused. It is a gift to be enjoyed and to be handled wisely. And wisdom itself is a gift of God. . . .
>
> Christian stewardship is rooted in the scriptures, is informed by instruction gleaned from the cosmic order, and flows from a communion with the Creator and a caring love for the creation. Christian stewardship is doing the Creator's will in caring for the earth and striving to preserve and restore the integrity, stability, and beauty of the created order, responding to creation's eager expectation of redemption. Christian stewardship is so living on earth that the Creator and creation are respected, the creation is preserved, brokenness is repaired, and harmony is restored. Christian stewardship seeks for the Creator's kingdom—a kingdom devoid of human arrogance, ignorance, and greed. Christian stewardship is so living on Earth that heaven will not be a shock to us.[10]

My hope and prayer is that this book has enabled my readers to have greater biblical insight into God's love and concern for creation and into the responsibility He has given all humans to be His caretakers over nature. I also pray that this journey has opened your eyes to the beauty and magnificence of creation, and that you will come to better love and enjoy nature as God intended it to be loved and enjoyed.

So, go outdoors and pay tribute to God by being a good steward over His creation. This can be a special delight to Christians because we know personally the Author of all things wild and beautiful.

TO NON-CHRISTIAN READERS

There is one more thing I would like to share, and this is specifically to non-Christian readers.

I know how you feel about nature, and I understand your skepticism about Christian environmentalism. However, I hope this book has convinced you that although Christians have often been negligent in protecting nature, so has *every* other culture and religious worldview at *every* stage of human history—including today. I hope you have also come to realize that biblical Christianity condemns environmental exploitation and abuse. The Bible teaches that the entire human race has a moral obligation to protect and care for creation. Moreover, in recent years, huge numbers of Christians have become aware of the seriousness of earth's mounting ecological and environmental problems, and they are advancing remedial solutions and advocating pro-environmental activities and legislation.

Now, I want to switch gears and share a few things about how I, as a non-Christian, came to be an advocate of Christian environmentalism.

For more than half my life I was *not* a Christian. Outside my family and closest friends, nature was the center of my life for thirty-six years. This changed abruptly in 1981. As I explained in the introduction, after I became a Christian my delight in nature almost immediately embraced an added delight in the Creator. From that point on, nature was no longer center stage in my life; God was. I also explained that this profound change did not lessen my love for nature or my desire to protect it; indeed, it enhanced it by giving meaning and purpose to those very things. I no longer love nature only for nature's sake and for how it gives *me* pleasure. I have a higher calling. I love and care for nature because the Creator loves and cares for it even more than I. God has graciously revealed wonderful things about Himself through what He designed and created.

What I didn't describe in the introduction was the remarkable spiritual journey this transition from a fervent devotee to nature to a committed follower of the Creator entailed. I want to share this journey with you now, because it made all the difference in my life. My story can be your story.

Before Christianity

The opening chapter of this grand journey is rooted in one of my earliest childhood memories. Shortly after World War II, my father acquired a mining claim in the desert area of the Tonto National Forest, in central Arizona. When I was four or five years old, I traveled with Mom and Dad from our home in Southern California to visit the mine. It was located on a hillside above a sweeping desert landscape. There was a small mill adjacent to the mine and a tiny one-room sheet metal shack. My parents slept on the only bed in the "cabin," and I slept on the floor. During the day I played outside, but at night, lying on the hard floor, I listened fearfully as woodrats scurried about the cabin looking for food and getting into mischief. It was a scary but thrilling experience to a small child—and my first conscious encounter with wildlife (such as it was).

I credit that trip into the arid wilderness as the beginning of a lifelong love for nature and all things wild, lonely, and beautiful—an enchantment that never weakened nor ever departed during all the ensuing years.

For much of my childhood, my family lived in small towns close to open country, farmlands, and dairies. My preferred playgrounds were always these "wild" lands: vegetated areas along irrigation canals, small woods surrounded by farmland, grassy meadows, brush-choked canyons, and any other wild habitat I could find. My friends and I always had favorite destinations to hike or ride our bikes to, places we called "Horned Toad Land," "Bullet Hill," and "The Old Oak Tree."

When I became a teenager, I left the outskirts of town every chance I could and camped and hiked with friends in remote locales. One of our parents would drive us to the desert or mountains, drop us off, and return to pick us up in a couple days. During those years I began to develop a special fondness for wildlife. When I was around fifteen or sixteen years old, I cut photographs out of magazines and books (ruining several books) to make my own field reference guide of animals living in the Southwest.

My wife and I were both nineteen when we married. Although she was a city girl, her love for the wilderness, hiking, and camping soon matched my own. After Earth Day in 1970, we became fervent advocates for ecological causes, especially preserving native habitats and protecting wildlife. We joined several pro-environmental groups and became involved in a wildlife rescue center. While representing the center, my wife went to public schools and gave wildlife programs; I wrote articles for the newsletter. During those years we also helped rescue and care for numerous injured and orphaned animals, and often brought them home to recuperate and prepare to be released back into the wilds. We hosted raccoons, squirrels, red-tailed hawks and other birds of prey, several varieties of songbirds and hummingbirds, and once a spotted skunk—who escaped from his cage and hid under a cupboard, refusing to come out. One day while I was shaving, a great horned owl sat on the toilet seat next to me, intensely watching—as owls do—every move I made.

In the mid-1970s, I started writing wildlife and ecology-related articles for magazines and newspapers, including, for two and a half years, a 1,400-word monthly column in a Sierra Club newspaper titled "Animal of the Month."

To this day, the majority of our vacations are spent in and about state and national parks and preserves. When I hike or mountain bike wild country, I still carry a camera with a telephoto lens. This lifelong relationship with nature recently bore additional fruit in a book I wrote on how to find and observe wildlife in a variety of natural habitats.[1]

Here's the point I want to make in sharing all this. I'm certain that few non-Christian environmentalists have a greater love for nature or greater eagerness to protect it than I. Being a Christian has not lessened my love for the wilderness or compromised my zeal to protect it. On the contrary, becoming a Christian enhanced my love and concern for nature.

After Becoming a Christian

In 1981, my wife, who was raised in a Christian home, decided to return to church with our kids. Not long afterward I tagged along, and within a short time my entire family were believers. Within a couple years, I returned to college and eventually earned a master's degree in Christian apologetics (a study in the defense of historic Christianity). I now had two great passions in my life. My old love for nature and my new love for the God who made it all. Although my family and I continued to hike and camp and spend most of our vacations in wild places, for the next twenty-five years I set aside writing about nature and ecology and focused on writing books and booklets and teaching classes that defended the Christian faith.

When I look back over my life before I became a Christian, I can't say that I ever purposely sought spiritual insight or solace in nature. But I did believe, as I shared in the previous chapter, that one could feel God's presence in wild places. It wasn't until *after* I became a Christian that I suspected my heartfelt kinship and fascination with nature was an extension of God's grace—a point of contact, if you will, that the Creator used to reach out to me! The Bible describes similar scenarios.

In a letter to Roman Christians, the apostle Paul wrote, "From the time the world was created, people have seen the earth and sky and all that God made. They can clearly see his invisible qualities—his eternal power and divine nature. So they have no excuse whatsoever for not knowing God."[2] When Paul lectured the Greek philosophers in Athens, he explained that God "made the world and everything in it" and "gives all men life and breath and everything else." After a few comments concerning God's sovereignty, he adds, "God did this so that men [and women] would seek him and perhaps reach out for him and find him, though he is not far from each one of us."[3]

I'm convinced that God's manifested grace is available to anyone willing to listen to His voice, calling to him or her in the wilderness. I see this demonstrated in the Bible in three ways.

First, God's revelation through creation confirms His existence and reveals certain essential traits of His divine nature. In particular, He maintains with loving care the earth and every living thing that dwells upon it. According to the Bible, this "general revelation" is available to all people, in every culture, and at every period throughout human history. It is an efficacious revelation; that is, it is able to successfully draw people to the Creator. This first point is well-established in the Bible.[4]

Second, I believe God's felt presence in creation is another way He communicates His desire for the human race to be caretakers over nature. What God loves and cares for, He wants people to love and care for. This divine commission was given to the first couple and passed down to all subsequent generations of human beings. We accept this task not just out of obedience, but also out of love for God. I've quoted numerous biblical passages throughout this book that demonstrate this fact, so it's unnecessary to probe it further.

There is a third way I believe God calls people to Himself through creation, one we haven't explored. Few theologians write about it, yet it may be God's most compelling outreach in nature to the human race.[5]

Yearning for Paradise

I believe one word best defines what I'm about to describe. It reveals a fundamental, deep-seated trait characteristic of human nature. The word is *nostalgia*.

The dictionary defines nostalgia as a fond, sentimental yearning for someplace far away, both in space and time—a place to which one can never return. The word, however, conveys more meaning than merely pleasant reminiscences of bygone days. It connotes a subconscious, "acute homesickness" for something more distant than the span of one's life or even the span of recorded human history.

If God placed this wonderful emotion in the human heart, there must be a reason. C. S. Lewis and other writers have pointed out that every natural or innate desire humans possess is a manifestation of a real and necessary human need. Physically, we crave food because we need to eat. Emotionally, we crave love because we were created to enjoy intimate relationships. We want respect and self-esteem because we were created with value. In the spiritual arena, we long for a relationship with God because He has placed this desire in our hearts. As fourth-century theologian Augustine said, "Thou [God] hast made us for Thyself, and our heart is restless until it rests in Thee."

Along this same idea, we can be confident that if we have a natural desire, an innate craving, for something for which this world offers no fulfillment, something *outside* this world will fulfill it. In other words, if there exists a longing for something this earth or human relationships cannot satisfy, God will satisfy it.

Here is what I'm suggesting. Feelings of nostalgia disclose a subconscious craving for *paradise*—homesickness for the perfect world God originally designed and intended to be our home, but which was lost in the horrible tragedy of the fall (see chapter 6). This intense yearning for a return to Eden can be set in motion through nature. When we experience the joy and peace of walking wild habitats, especially when we feel God's presence, perhaps without realizing it, I believe we are actually longing to return to paradise lost.

The Bible teaches, as we saw in chapter 8, that God placed Adam and Eve in a perfect garden called Eden. It was a *natural* environment. It was free of death, predation, natural disasters, and harmful plants and animals. The first couple lived in a close personal relationship with their Creator and in perfect harmony with nature. Unfortunately, because of their heartbreaking rebellion against God and consequent estrangement, the first humans were banished from the garden and thrust into a hostile physical environment, not unlike that which people live in to this day. Nevertheless, although God removed us from the garden, He didn't remove our latent memory of it or the desire to return.

The good news in this sad saga is that paradise lost can become paradise regained. Many passages in Scripture reveal that at the end of this present age God will redeem and heal nature and return it to its original pristine state, as it existed before the fall.[6] It will be a place free of abuse and the wounds of environmental exploitation.

As pointed out, however, nostalgia is longing for a place to which we *can't* return. We cannot go back to our former paradisaical home. On the other hand, because God has not given us any desires that do not have a fulfillment, this yearning for Eden will be fulfilled in a future, renewed "new heaven and earth" where nature will be restored to its former glory.[7] Thus, on a spiritual level, nostalgia actually looks forward, not backward. The Bible reveals that this redeemed and regenerated nature here on earth is the guaranteed eternal destiny of everyone who loves God and receives His Son as personal Savior.

In the meantime, this perfect nature can be partially glimpsed in this life by exploring and experiencing wild habitats, and by enjoying and loving the Creator who made and maintains them.[8] When I sit in a lonely spot and watch the sublime beauty of a glorious sunrise, hike across a desert valley on a full moon night, feel the power and energy of a high mountain thunderstorm; when I hike alongside a meandering herd of bison in Yellowstone National Park, gaze across Zion canyon from the lofty summit of Angel's Landing, wander within the solemn three hundred foot redwood forest cathedrals in north coastal California, or even stare in wonder at the amazing design and complexity of the insects and spiders living in my yard—it's easy to sense the presence of the One who made them all. Yet, all this magnificence is but a hint of what's to come; the flavor of mountain water, but not the spring; the scent of a flower, but not the rose.

Wilderness, then, is a mystical foretaste of paradise lost; an image or symbol of the original divine garden with all its joy and peace and unspoiled beauty. In God's timing the wilderness you and I know and love will become transformed. The dim memory of Eden hovering in the recesses of our minds will someday become a living reality.[9]

This is the marvelous outcome of opening your heart to God in the wilderness. It will shine a golden light on a path that can lead to a personal, life-changing relationship with the Creator. By sincerely receiving Jesus Christ and following Him, you can know that your dreams of a permanent home in unspoiled nature will one day materialize. You will walk through pristine wilderness—as peaceful and bountiful as a garden. You will experience sights, sounds, smells, and textures only dimly reflected in the wilderness you now love. But, as in the conclusion of Robert Frost's memorable poem, you have a choice.

> Two roads diverged in a wood, and I,
> I took the one less traveled by,
> And that has made all the difference.

I pray you will take the road to Jesus Christ because it will make all the difference. Healed and glorious nature awaits, ruled over by the Lord of the universe. I hope I'll see you there.

ENDNOTES

Introduction

1. For example, I recently heard the host of a nationally broadcast conservative talk radio program make the statement that recycling is a "waste of time" and has only "psychological benefits." Presumably, he meant that recycling makes us feel good because we are doing something that is ostensibly positive for the environment, but is not actually helpful. In fact this isn't true. According to an EPA report, "Municipal Solid Waste Generation, Recycling, and Disposal in the United States: Facts and Figures for 2007," Americans annually generate about 251 million tons of trash and only recycle about 82 million tons. Most of this waste (55 to 65 percent) is generated as residential waste, the majority being recyclable products (paper, wood, metals, plastics, and so on). Paper products alone account for 33.9 percent of residential waste. The report adds, "Every ton of mixed paper recycled can save the energy equivalent of 185 gallons of gas" (www.epa.gov/epawaste/nonhaz/municipal/pubs/msw07-fs.pdf). Since many of the products humanity consumes are finite—including the petroleum, aluminum, and copper used in many recyclable items—it's beyond comprehension to me how anyone can believe that recycling has only psychological benefits.

2. Stephen Rand, "Love Your Neighbor As Yourself," in *The Care of Creation: Focusing Concern and Action*, ed. R. J. Berry (Downers Grove, IL: InterVarsity, 2000), 145.

One: What Ever Happened to the Environmental Movement?

1. For a historical survey of the environmental movement in the United States, see *American Environmentalism*, ed. Greg Barton (San Diego: Greenhaven, 2002).

2. Hope Ryden, *God's Dog* (New York: Coward, McCann & Geoghegan, 1975), 250.

3. Martin Griffith, "Coyote Hunt Has Activists Outraged," *San Diego Union-Tribune,* January 9, 2010.

4. Peter Matthiessen, *Wildlife in America*, rev. ed. (New York: Viking, 1987), 197–98. Also see Joseph Wood Krutch, *The Voice of the Desert* (New York: William Sloane Associates, 1962), 198.

5. Richard Louv, *Last Child in the Woods: Saving Our Children from Nature-Deficit Disorder* (Chapel Hill, NC: Algonquin Books, 2005), 276.

6. Ibid., 270, 276.

7. Richard Louv, "Marking the End of Conservation," *San Diego Union-Tribune,* November 8, 2005, opinion section.

8. According to a Kaiser Family Foundation survey of 2,002 eight- to eighteen-year-olds, the average young person spends more than seven and half hours *daily* using some form of media (listening to music, TV and movies, video games, and "hanging out online"). Greg Toppo, "Kids' Electronic Media Use Jumps to 53 Hours a Week," *USA Today,* January 20, 2010, http://www.usatoday.com/tech/news/2010-01-20-1Avideokids20_ST_N.htm.

9. Oliver R. W. Pergams and Patricia A. Zaradic, "Evidence for a Fundamental and Pervasive Shift Away from Nature-Based Recreation," *PNAS* 105, no. 7 (February 19, 2008): 2295–2300, doi:10.1073/pnas.0709893105.

10. Ibid., 2299.

11. Louv, *Last Child in the Woods*, 16, 19.

12. Ibid., 270.

13. Ibid., 3, 43.

14. Ibid., chapter 8.

15. See www.greenexercise.org. The report also includes links to similar research.

16. Gary Paul Nabhan, "Cultural Parallax in Viewing North American Habitats," in *Worldviews, Religion, and the Environment: A Global Anthology*, ed. Richard C. Foltz (Belmont, CA: Wadsworth, 2003), 109.

17. Ibid.

18. Pergams and Zaradic, "Evidence for a Fundamental and Pervasive Shift," 2295.

19. "Pollution: Keep America Beautiful—Iron Eyes Cody (1961–1983)," http://www.staging.adcouncil.org/default.aspx?id=132.

20. Richard T. Wright, "The *Declaration* Under Siege," in *The Care of Creation: Focusing Concern and Action*, ed. R. J. Berry (Downers Grove, IL: InterVarsity, 2000), 79.

21. Michael S. Northcott, "The Spirit of Environmentalism," in *The Care of Creation*, 173–74.

22. I. Howard Marshall, "Commitment to Creation," in *The Care of Creation*, 95.

Two: Are Christians Responsible for the Environmental Crisis?

1. Lynn White Jr., "The Historical Roots of Our Ecologic Crisis," *Science* 155, no. 3767 (March 10, 1967): 1205, doi:10.1126/science.155.3767.1203.

2. Ibid., 1204.

3. Ibid., 1205.

4. Ibid.

5. Ibid., 1206.

6. Ibid., 1205.

7. Ibid.

8. Donald Worster, *Nature's Economy: The Roots of Ecology* (New York: Anchor/Doubleday, 1979), 27.

9. Eric G. Bolen and William L. Robinson, *Wildlife Ecology and Management* (New York: Macmillan, 1984), 5–6. Note: The "hundreds of generations" that the authors speak of would push back the influence of Genesis to 7000 or 8000 BC.

10. Peter Singer, *Animal Liberation* (New York: New York Review, 1975), 203–4, 208–9.

11. Jean Dorst, *Before Nature Dies*, trans. Constance D. Sherman (Baltimore: Penguin, 1971), 19.

12. Jeremy Rifkin with Ted Howard, *Entropy: A New World View* (New York: Viking, 1980), 48.

13. Robin Attfield, *The Ethics of Environmental Concern* (Oxford: Basil Blackwell, 1983), 34.

14. Dorst, *Before Nature Dies*, 26–27.

15. Ibid., 32.

16. Ibid., 33.

17. See René Dubos, *A God Within* (New York: Charles Scribner's Sons, 1972), chapter 8.

18. Jacques Ellul, *The Technological Society*, trans. John Wilkinson (New York: Alfred A. Knopf, 1964), 35.

19. Peter Gay, *The Enlightenment: An Interpretation: The Rise of Modern Paganism*, vol. 1 (New York: W. W. Norton, 1977), 248.

20. Langdon Gilkey, *Religion and the Scientific Future* (Macon, GA: Mercer University Press, 1981), 7.

21. For a survey of the emergence of secular humanism, see my book *Christianity on the Offense: Responding to the Beliefs and Assumptions of Spiritual Seekers* (Grand Rapids: Kregel, 1998), chapter 11.

Three: Are Non-Christians Religions More Environmentally Responsible Than Christianity?

1. Ghillean T. Prance, "The Earth Under Threat," in *The Care of Creation: Focusing Concern and Action*, ed. R. J. Berry (Downers Grove, IL: InterVarsity, 2000), 117.

2. Tony Campolo, *How to Rescue the Earth Without Worshiping Nature* (Nashville: Thomas Nelson, 1992), 99, emphasis original.

3. Shepard Krech III, *The Ecological Indian: Myth and History* (New York: W. W. Norton, 1999), 22.

4. T. C. McLuhan, *Touch the Earth: A Self-Portrait of Indian Existence* (New York: Promontory, 1971), 1–2.

5. Gary Paul Nabhan, "Cultural Parallax in Viewing North American Habitats" in *Worldviews, Religion, and the Environment: A Global Anthology,* ed. Richard C. Foltz (Belmont, CA: Wadsworth, 2003), 108.

6. Krech, *The Ecological Indian*, 108. Chapter 4 gives a detailed account of how fire was used by Native Americans across the continent.

7. George Catlin, *North American Indians: Being Letters and Notes on Their Manners, Customs, and Conditions, Written During Eight Years' Travel Amongst the Wildest Tribes of Indians in North America, 1832–1939*, 2 vols.

(Philadelphia: Learly, Stuart, 1913), vol. 1, excerpted in "America Needs a National Park," *American Environmentalism*, ed. Greg Barton (San Diego: Greenhaven, 2002), 172. See also Krech, *The Ecological Indian*, chapter 5.

8. Krech, *The Ecological Indian*, 215–20.

9. Quoted in Donald Worster, *Nature's Economy: The Roots of Ecology* (Garden City, NY: Anchor/Doubleday, 1979), 171.

10. Estimates vary on the worldwide population of indigenous people. For a list of various population estimates and their sources, see Adherents.com, http://www.adherents.com/Na/Na_534.html.

11. *The Perennial Dictionary of World Religions*, gen. ed. Keith Crim (New York: Harper & Row, 1981), 37.

12. Edward G. Newing, "Religions of Pre-Literary Societies," in *The World's Religions*, ed. Sir Norman Anderson (Grand Rapids: Eerdmans, 1980), 39.

13. Harold E. Driver, *Indians of North America*, 2nd ed. (Chicago: University of Chicago Press, 1970), 397.

14. Paul G. Hiebert, R. Daniel Shaw, and Tite Tiénou, *Understanding Folk Religion* (Grand Rapids: Baker, 1999), 87.

15. Newing, "Religions of Pre-Literary Societies," 33.

16. Hiebert, Shaw, and Tiénou, *Understanding Folk Religion*, 78.

17. Denise Lardner Carmody and John Carmody, *Religion: The Great Questions* (New York: Seabury, 1983), 143.

18. Estimates vary. See "Statistics," The Pluralism Project at Harvard University © 1997–2011, http://pluralism.org/resources/statistics/index.php.

19. O. P. Dwivedi, "Dharmic Ecology" in *Worldviews, Religion, and the Environment*, ed. Richard C. Foltz (Belmont, CA: Wadsworth/Thomson Learning, 2003), 119–20.

20. Jean Dorst, *Before Nature Dies*, trans. Constance D. Sherman (Baltimore: Penguin, 1971), 26.

21. David N. Livingstone, "The Church Is to Blame," *Christianity Today*, April 4, 1994, 25.

22. Stephen Neill, *Christian Faith & Other Faiths* (Downers Grove, IL: InterVarsity, 1984), 147.

23. Ian Harris, "Ecological Buddhism?" in *Worldviews, Religion, and the*

Environment, ed. Richard C. Foltz (Belmont, CA: Wadsworth/Thomas Learning, 2003), 176.

24. Carmody and Carmody, *Religion: The Great Questions*, 152.

25. An example of true stewardship would be protecting endangered wildlife from extinction by restricting land development in spite of potential economic profits.

26. Harris, "Ecological Buddhism?" 177–78.

27. Loren Wilkinson, "The Making of the *Declaration*," in *The Care of Creation: Focusing Concern and Action*, ed. R. J. Berry (Downers Grove, IL: InterVarsity, 2000), 53.

28. There is, however, reason to be concerned about the growing popularity of nature religions. Professor of Religion and Nature at the University of Florida, Bron Taylor, refers to "religions that consider nature to be sacred, imbued with intrinsic value, and worthy of reverent care" as "dark green religion." He doesn't suggest they will eventually become a universal, monolithic religion, but he does point out that "such religion is becoming increasingly important in global environmental politics," and that "it may even inspire the emergence of a global, civic, earth religion." *Dark Green Religion: Nature Spirituality and the Planetary Future* (Los Angeles: University of California Press, 2010), ix–x.

29. For a summary of radical environmentalism see ibid., ch. 4.

30. Tom Dunkel, "Why Is the Nature Conservancy's Ecologist in Chief So Concerned About Humanity?" *Nature Conservancy Magazine* 61, no. 1 (Spring 2011): 32.

31. Peter Kareiva, "Balancing the Needs of People and Nature," *Nature Conservancy Magazine* 61, no. 1 (Spring 2011): 38, emphasis in original.

32. Dunkel, "Why Is The Nature Conservancy's Ecologist in Chief So Concerned About Humanity?" 37.

Four: The Environmental Crisis: Fact or Fiction?

1. In reality, the ostrich will sometimes lie on the ground with its neck outstretched to escape detection. This gave rise to the notion that they bury their heads in the sand when frightened.

2. Tanya Mannes, "Sand Gift Will Help Replenish Beaches," *San Diego Union-Tribune,* January 9, 2009.

3. Daniel James Devine, "Clouding the Debate," *World,* August 14, 2010, 50.

4. Katharine Hayhoe and Andrew Farley, *A Climate for Change: Global Warming Facts for Faith-Based Decisions* (New York: Faith Words, 2009), 71. See also Peter T. Doran and Maggie Kendall Zimmerman, "Examining the Scientific Consensus on Climate Change," *Eos, Transactions American Geophysical Union* 90, no. 3 (2009): 22, doi:10.1029/2009EO030002.

5. E. Calvin Beisner, "Deep Ecology, Neopaganism & Global Warming," in *On Global Wizardry; Techniques of Pagan Spirituality and a Christian Response*, ed. Peter Jones (Escondido, CA: Main Entry Editions, 2010), 183.

6. A good example of how faulty logic can lead to erroneous conclusions is illustrated in C. Wayne Mayhall's critique of Al Gore's *An Inconvenient Truth.* See C. Wayne Mayhall, "A Summary Critique: 'You Can't Handle "The Inconvenient Truth"!'" *Christian Research Journal* 30, no. 4 (2004): 44–48.

7. The earth's climate depends on the occurrence of a *natural* "greenhouse effect." Light from the sun heats the earth's surface. Some of this energy is radiated back into space. However, water vapor, carbon dioxide, ozone, methane, and nitrous oxide in the atmosphere absorb much of this heat and reradiate it back to earth—much like the window panes in a greenhouse allow light to enter but prevent the heat from radiating out. Without this protective barrier, the earth's average surface temperature would be an estimated 60°F cooler. The assumption among global warming advocates is that increased emissions from human activities have raised the concentration of these gases in the atmosphere, causing higher levels of heat energy to be trapped and radiated back to earth. Supposedly, this is raising the planet's overall temperature.

8. Thomas R. Karl, Jerry M. Melillo, and Thomas C. Peterson, eds., U.S. Global Change Research Program, "Global Climate Change Impacts in the United States," (New York: Cambridge University Press, 2009), http://downloads.globalchange.gov/usimpacts/pdfs/climate-impacts-report.pdf.

9. Beisner claims that most assumptions about global warming are based on

computer models which, he says, "do not *describe* [and] cannot *predict,* and even fail to retrodict past climate changes without miltiple, enormous, *ad hoc* adjustments." "Deep Ecology," 183, emphasis in original.

10. Karl, Melillo, and Peterson, "Global Climate Change Impacts," 14.

11. "Climate Change 2007: Synthesis Report: Summary for Policy Makers," 8, http://www.ipcc.ch/pdf/assessment-report/ar4/syr/ar4_syr_spm.pdf.

12. Ibid., 17, emphasis in original.

13. Karl, Melillo, and Peterson, "Global Climate Change Impacts," 16.

14. U.S. Environmental Protection Agency, "State of Knowledge," http://www.epa.gov/climatechange/science/stateofknowledge.html (last updated November 29, 2011).

15. Hayhoe and Farley, *A Climate for Change,* 39.

16. Another evidence of global warming is the increase and severity of wildfires in Australia, United States, and other parts of the world. In July of 2007, more than seventy wildfires were burning in twelve Western states. Researchers at Scripps Institution of Oceanography, University of California, San Diego, and at the University of Arizona did "the most systematic analysis to date of the possible reasons for the rapid rise in wildfires since the late 1980s." Other scientists from UCSD compiled data from 1,166 western wildfires that each burned at least a thousand acres between 1970 and 2003. The researchers concluded, among other things, that the dramatic increase in wildfires since the late 1980s is "one of the first big indicators of climate-change impacts in the continental United States." In other words, if global warming is occurring, one of the serious ecological impacts is larger and more frequent wildfires of greater duration. Supposedly, due to climate changes, spring comes earlier in the West, summers are hotter and longer, and brush is dryer and more flammable. Bruce Lieberman, "Heat Adding Fuel to Fires, Study Suggests," *San Diego Union-Tribune,* July 7, 2006.

17. Beisner provides other sources that challenge human-caused global warming. See Beisner, "Deep Ecology," 184–85.

18. Quoted in Devine, "Clouding the Debate," 50. Other evangelical climate scientists strongly argue that climate change is due specifically to human-generated greenhouse gases. Katharine Hayhoe and Andrew Farley make a

powerful and compelling scientific case for human-caused global warming in *A Climate for Change.*

19. Joseph Kahn and Jim Yardly, "As China Roars, Pollution Reaches Deadly Extremes," *New York Times*, August 26, 2007, 5, http://www.nytimes .com/2007/08/26/world/asia/26china.html?pagewanted=print.

20. David Periman, "CO_2 Turning the Oceans Acidic," *San Diego Union-Tribune,* July 13, 2006. Research studies on this topic are available online.

21. Sierra Club, "Sprawl Losses Staggering," http://www.sierraclub.org/sprawl /articles/USDAreport.asp (accessed December 15, 2010).

22. Calvin B. DeWitt, "Creation's Environmental Challenge to Evangelical Christianity," in *The Care of Creation: Focusing Concern and Action*, ed. R. J. Berry (Downers Grove, IL: InterVarsity, 2000), 61.

23. Food and Agriculture Organization of the United Nations, "Deforestation Continues at an Alarming Rate," FAO Newsroom, November 14, 2005, http://www.fao.org/newsroom/en/news/2005/1000127/index.html.

24. The Food and Agriculture Organization of the United Nations (FAO) released these figures in its 2005 *Global Forest Resources Assessment.* See Rhett A. Butler, "United States Has 7th Highest Rate of Primary Forest Loss," Mongabay.com, November 16, 2005, http://news.mongabay.com/2005 /1116-forests.html.

25. "Global Deforestation."

26. Ibid.

27. Greg Barton, ed. *American Environmentalism* (San Diego: Greenhavens, 2002), 135.

28. Earth Watch, "Amazon Deforestation," *San Diego Union-Tribune,* June 12, 2008. Many research articles on this topic are available online.

29. Gerald Urquhart, Walter Chomentowski, David Skole, and Chris Barber, "Tropical Deforestation," *Earth Observatory,* http://earthobservatory .nasa.gov/Features/Deforestation/tropical_deforestation_2001.pdf.

30. Rhett A. Butler, "Atmospheric Role of Forests," Mongabay.com, January 4, 2009, http://rainforests.mongabay.com/0907.htm.

31. G. Serrano, "Killer Inhabitants of the Rainforest," Trends Updates, January 4, 2009, http://trendsupdates.com/killer-inhabitants-of-the-rainforests/.

32. Young earth creationists believe that most prehistoric animals became extinct during or shortly after the worldwide flood due to drastic climatic changes and other related causes. They offer fossil and geological evidences to support their view. Interested readers should contact the Institute for Creation Research at www.icr.org or Answers in Genesis at www.AnswersinGenesis.org.

33. Julia Whitty, "Animal Extinction—the Greatest Threat to Mankind," *Independent*, April 30, 2007, http://www.independent.co.uk/environment /animal-extinction--the-greatest-threat-to-mankind-397939.html.

34. Ibid.

35. Ibid. The World Conservation Union's Red List can be accessed at http:// www.iucnredlist.org

36. Whitty, "Animal Extinction."

37. Ibid.

38. Ibid.

39. See the Smithsonian Institute, "The Passenger Pigeon," http://www.si.edu /encyclopedia_Si/nmnh/passpig.htm.

40. Joseph R. Mendelson III, et al., "Confronting Amphibian Declines and Extinctions," *Science* 313, no. 5783, (July 7, 2006): 48, doi: 10.1126/science .1128396.

41. John Biemer, "Experts Warn of Total Amphibian Extinction, Fearing Cataclysm," *San Diego Union-Tribune*, July 7, 2006.

Five: Creation

1. Denise Lardner Carmody and John Carmody, *Religions: The Great Questions* (New York: Seabury, 1983), 30.

2. By "theology of nature," I mean a systematic analysis of all relevant Bible passages and teachings that contribute to developing an environmental doctrine.

3. C. S. Lewis, *Reflections on the Psalms* (New York: Harcourt Brace Jovanovich, 1958), 81–83.

4. Loren Wilkinson, "The Uneasy Conscience of the Human Race: Rediscovering Creation in the 'Environmental' Movement," in *God and Culture: Essays in Honor of Carl F. H. Henry* (Grand Rapids: Eerdmans, 1993), 312.

5. Guillermo Gonzales and Jay W. Richards, *The Privileged Planet: How Our Place in the Cosmos Is Designed for Discovery* (Washington, DC: Regnery, 2004). This book provides conclusive scientific evidence that planet earth was carefully designed to support life, especially human life.

6. Peter Singer, *Animal Liberation: A New Ethics for Our Treatment of Animals* (New York: A New York Review Book, distributed by Random House, 1975), 209.

7. C. F. D. Moule, *Man and Nature in the New Testament* (Philadelphia: Fortress, 1967), 1.

8. Susan P. Bratton, *Christianity, Wilderness and Wildlife: The Original Desert Solitaire* (Scranton: University of Scranton Press, 2009), 298.

9. William Dyrness, "Stewardship of the Earth in the Old Testament," in *Tending the Garden: Essays on the Gospel and the Earth,* ed. Wesley Granberg-Michaelson, (Grand Rapids: Eerdmans, 1987), 63.

Six: The Fall

1. Ron Sider, "Courageous Nonviolence," *Christianity Today*, December 2007, 44. Sider cites statistics from Jonathan Glover, *Humanity: A Moral History of the 20th Century* and R. J. Rummel, *Statistics of Democide.*

2. Alfred, Lord Tennyson, *In Memoriam.*

3. Some people argue that Adam's descendants should not be punished for Adam's sin. There are three ways to respond to this. First, Adam was the representative head of the human race; his name is a general term for *mankind.* Just as the decisions made by a president affect all people subject to his rule, so Adam's decision to rebel against God affected all humanity. Second, sin can be pictured as a genetic disease. When Adam fell, he became infected with a communicable disease (a sin nature) that was passed to all his descendants—which includes everyone who ever lived. Third, when Adam sinned he not only represented us, he acted in the same way people do today and always have. All people disobey God (sin—Rom. 3:23). Thus, all people are accountable to God for their *own* sins and subject to the consequence of their own behaviors (Rom. 6:23). Hence, we need a Savior (Rom. 8:1).

4. Eric Charles Rust, *Nature—Garden or Desert? An Essay in Environmental Theology* (Waco, TX: Word, 1971), 28.

5. William Lane Craig, *Reasonable Faith: Christian Truth and Apologetics* (Wheaton, IL: Crossway, 1994), 91. Also see Dan Story, *The Christian Combat Manual: Helps for Defending Your Faith: A Handbook for Practical Apologetics* (Chattanooga: AMG, 2007), 84–87.

Seven: Redemption

1. H. Paul Santmire, *Brother Earth: Nature, God, and Ecology in Time of Crisis* (New York: Thomas Nelson, 1970), 110.

2. Ibid., 163.

3. Hanlee H. Barnette, *The Church and the Ecological Crisis* (Grand Rapids: Eerdmans, 1972), 40.

4. Some theologians argue that 2 Peter 3:10, 12 teaches a cataclysmic ending to the present earth, perhaps by nuclear war, a collision between the earth and an asteroid or comet, or some other cosmic event. Religious professor Steven Bouma-Prediger comments on this:

> To put it bluntly, this verse represents perhaps the most egregious mistranslation in the entire New Testament. . . . The [Greek] text states that after a refiner's fire of purification (v. 7), the new earth will be *found*, not burned up. The earth will be *discovered*, not destroyed. John Calvin's take on this text is instructive. Summarizing his interpretation, Susan Schreiner states, "Therefore, in Calvin's view, the fires of judgment will not destroy creation but will purify its original and enduring substance. With this argument, Calvin portrayed God as faithful to his original creation. Just as God brought the cosmos into being, closely governs and restrains its natural forces, so too he will renew and transform its original substance." This text does not refer to the Rapture. It is not about the destruction of creation. It refers, rather, to the purification and renewal of creation. As Thomas Finger insists in his careful study of this text, "The main emphasis of the text is that everything will be scrutinized or assessed

by God, and not necessarily destroyed." Thus, 2 Peter 3 rightly rendered speaks of a basic continuity rather than discontinuity of this world with the next. (Emphasis in original.)

It should be added that even if nature is literally destroyed and recreated, it does not remove our obligation before God to care for and work for its healing in this life. Steven Bouma-Prediger, *For the Beauty of the Earth: A Christian Vision for Creation Care*, 2nd ed. (Grand Rapids: Baker Academic, 2010), 68–69.

5. I agree with the commentary in the NIV *Quest Study Bible* that in Isaiah 65:17, "it's much more likely that [Isaiah] was using the word create to mean transform." Other passages that refer to a recreated new earth include Isaiah 35:1–7; 41:17–20; 43:19–21; 66:22; 2 Peter 3:13; Revelation 22:1–6.

6. Santmire, *Brother Earth*, 109.

7. Bouma-Prediger, *For the Beauty of the Earth*, 118.

8. Francis A. Schaeffer, *Pollution and the Death of Man: A Christian View of Ecology* (Wheaton, IL: Tyndale House, 1981), 66.

9. Ibid., 68–69.

10. Ibid., 69.

11. Loren Wilkinson, "Interlude: Joy or Despair" in *Earthkeeping: Christian Stewardship of Natural Resources*, ed. Loren Wilkinson (Grand Rapids: Eerdmans, 1980), 97.

Eight: Stewardship

1. I provide a theological and systematic study of the doctrine of the Trinity in my books, *Defending Your Faith: Reliable Answers for a New Generation of Seekers and Skeptics* (Grand Rapids: Kregel, 1997), chapter 8, and *The Christian Combat Manual: Helps for Defending Your Faith: A Handbook for Practical Apologetics* (Chattanooga: AMG, 2007), chapter 22.

2. H. Paul Santmire, "Reflections on the Alleged Ecological Bankruptcy of Western Theology," in *Ethics for Environment: Three Religious Strategies*, ed. Dave Steffenson, Walter J. Herrscher, and Robert S. Cook (Green Bay: UWGB Ecumenical Center, 1973), 32.

3. Henlee H. Barnette, *The Church and the Ecological Crisis* (Grand Rapids: Eerdmans, 1972), 79.

4. John Stott, *Issues Facing Christians Today*, 4th edition (Grand Rapids: Zondervan, 2006), 154.

5. Francis A. Schaeffer, *Pollution and the Death of Man: The Christian View of Ecology* (Wheaton, IL: Tyndale, 1981), 69.

6. C. F. D. Moule, *Man and Nature in the New Testament* (Philadelphia: Fortress, 1967), 14.

7. Barnette, *The Church and the Ecological Crisis*, 81.

8. Carl F. H. Henry, "Stewardship of the Environment" in *Applying the Scriptures: Papers from ICBI Summit III*, ed. Kenneth S. Kantzer (Grand Rapids: Zondervan, 1987), 477.

9. Geoffrey W. Bromiley, "Eschatology: The Meaning of the End," in *God and Culture: Essays in Honor of Carl F. H. Henry*, ed. D. A. Carson and John D. Woodbridge (Grand Rapids: Eerdmans, 1993), 82.

10. Warren W. Wiersbe, *The Bible Exposition Commentary: An Exposition of the New Testament Comprising the Entire "BE" Series*, vol. 2 (Colorado Springs: Victor, 1989), 584, 601.

Ten: America's Emerging Ecological Conscience

1. Greg Barton, ed., *American Environmentalism* (San Diego: Greenhaven, 2002), 39.

2. Donald Worster, *Nature's Economy: The Roots of Ecology* (New York: Anchor, 1979), 81.

3. Ibid., 83–84.

4. H. Paul Santmire, *Brother Earth: Nature, God, and Ecology in Time of Crisis* (New York: Thomas Nelson, 1970), 17.

5. J. Gray Sweeney, *Masterpieces of Western American Art* (New York: M & M, 1991), 158.

6. Worster, *Nature's Economy*, 86.

7. Loren Wilkinson, "The North American Experience" in *Earthkeeping: Christian Stewardship of Natural Resources*, ed. Loren Wilkinson (Grand Rapids: Eerdmans, 1980), 140.

8. Worster, *Nature's Economy*. Chapter 12 provides a history of the Dust Bowl experiences and its causes.

9. Frederick Elder, *Crisis in Eden: A Religious Study of Man and the Environment* (New York: Abingdon, 1970), 91.

10. Aldo Leopold, *A Sand County Almanac and Sketches Here and There* (New York: Oxford University Press, 1949), 201–26.

11. Worster, *Nature's Economy*, 284.

12. Ibid., 287.

13. Leopold, *Sand County Almanac*, 203.

14. Ibid., 204.

15. Ibid.

16. Ibid., 203.

17. Worster, *Nature's Economy*, 288–89.

18. Christopher D. Stone, *Should Trees Have Standing? Toward Legal Rights for Natural Objects* (New York: Avon, 1975). In 1996 Stone published an updated and expanded edition that gives a more thorough treatment than the original edition. See Christopher D. Stone, *Should Trees Have Standing? and Other Essays on Law, Morals and the Environment* (Dobbs Ferry, NY: Oceana, 1996).

19. Ibid., 1975 edition, 25.

20. Ibid., 55.

Eleven: Is Environmental Exploitation Sin?

1. Bob Diddlebock, "Urban Poaching," *Time*, October 22, 2007, 53–54.

2. Steven Bouma-Prediger, *For the Beauty of the Earth: A Christian Vision for Creation Care*, 2nd ed. (Grand Rapids: Baker Academic, 2010), 148.

Twelve: Bible-Based Environmental Ethics

1. Quoted in *The Green Bible* (San Francisco: HarperCollins, 2008), 105.

2. Tony Campolo, *How to Rescue the Earth Without Worshiping Nature* (Nashville: Thomas Nelson, 1992), 23.

3. Loren Wilkinson, "Who's in Charge" in *Earthkeeping: Christian Stewardship of Natural Resources*, ed. Loren Wilkinson (Grand Rapids: Eerdmans, 1980), 216, 218.

4. *The Complete Word Study Dictionary, New Testament*, gen. ed. Spiros Zodhiates (Chattanooga: AMG, 1993), s.v. "agape."

5. Wilkinson, "Who's in Charge," 215.

6. Ibid.

7. Denise Lardner Carmody and John Carmody, *Religions: The Great Questions* (New York: Seabury, 1983), 131–32.

8. Francis A. Schaeffer, *Pollution and the Death of Man: The Christian View of Ecology* (Wheaton, IL: Tyndale, 1970), 90.

Thirteen: The Church in Action

1. Elsewhere I have examined the inability of secular worldviews, in particular naturalistic evolution and atheism, to develop an objective basis for moral behavior. See Dan Story, *The Christian Combat Manual: Helps for Defending Your Faith: A Handbook for Practical Apologetics* (Chattanooga: AMG, 2007), chapter 18.

2. John T. Houghton, "Our Common Future," in *The Care of Creation*, R. J. Berry, ed. (Downers Grove, IL: InterVarsity, 2000), 130.

3. Frederick Elder, *Crisis in Eden: A Religious Study of Man and Environment* (New York: Abingdon, 1970), 160–61.

4. Pew Research Center, "Faith-Based Funding Backed, But Church-State Doubts Abound," April 10, 2001, Section IV: Religion in American Life, http://www.people-press.org/2001/04/10/section-iv-religion-in-american-life/.

5. Barna Update, "Evangelicals Go 'Green' with Caution," September 22, 2008, http://www.barna.org/barna-update/article/13-culture/23-evangelicals-go-qgreenq-with-caution?q=evangelical.

6. "For the Health of the Nation: An Evangelical Call to Civic Responsibility" (National Association of Evangelicals, 2004), http://www.nae.net/images/content/For_The_Health_Of_The_Nation.pdf.

7. Cindy Crosby, "Christian Colleges' Green Revolution," *Christianity Today*, May 2007, 52.

8. Michelle A. Vu, "Evangelicals, U.S. Government Promote Green Churches," *Christian Post*, November 8, 2007, http://www.christianpost.com/news/evangelicals-u-s-govt-promote-green-churches-30004.

9. Mary Hurn Korte, "Environmental Education, Ethics, and Evidential Apologetics," in *Tough-minded Christianity*, ed. William Dembski and Thomas Schirrmacher (Nashville, TN: B & H, 2008), 517–18.

10. Tri Robinson with Jason Chatraw, *Saving God's Green Earth: Rediscovering the Church's Responsibility to Environmental Stewardship* (Norcross, GA: Ampelon, 2006).

11. Calvin B. DeWitt, *Earth-Wise: A Biblical Response to Environmental Issues*, 2nd ed. (Grand Rapids: Faith Alive Christian Resources, 2007), chapters 5 and 6. Another resource for mobilizing environmental programs in the local church is Edward R. Brown, *Our Father's World: Mobilizing the Church to Care for Creation* (Downers Grove, IL: InterVarsity, 2008).

12. I wrote a book designed to help people find and observe wildlife in a variety of natural habitats, from wilderness areas to city parks. It can be a great aid to enjoying and experiencing outdoor activities with the entire family. See Dan Story, *Where Wild Things Live: Wildlife Watching Techniques and Adventures* (Happy Camp, CA: Naturegraph, 2009).

13. Robinson, *Saving God's Green Earth*, 21–22.

14. See the website for 1 Bag at a Time, http://www.onebagatatime.com/.

15. "Numbers," *Time*, April 28, 2008, 23, http://www.time.com/time/magazine/article/0,9171,1731890,00html.

16. Steven Bouma-Prediger, *For the Beauty of the Earth: A Christian Vision for Creation Care*, 2nd ed. (Grand Rapids: Baker Academic, 2010), 160.

Fourteen: Ecological Evangelism

1. Dan Story, "Should Christians Be Environmentalists?" *Christian Research Journal* 22, no. 4 (2010): 20–27.

2. Dan Story, *Engaging the Closed Minded: Presenting Your Faith to the Confirmed Unbeliever* (Grand Rapids: Kregel, 1999), ch. 6.

3. Rick Cornish, *5 Minute Apologist: Maximum Truth in Minimum Time* (Colorado Springs: NavPress, 2005), 17. See also Joseph Popiolkowsky and Adrienne Lewis, "Losing Their Religion," *USA Today*, March 9, 2004.

4. Stephen Rand, "Love Your Neighbor As Yourself," in *The Care of Creation:*

Focusing Concern and Action, ed. R. J. Berry (Downers Grove, IL: InterVarsity, 2000), 45.

5. Ibid.

6. Edward R. Brown, *Our Father's World: Mobilizing the Church to Care for Creation*, 2nd ed. (Downers Grove, IL: InterVarsity Press, 2008), 154.

7. Tri Robinson with Jason Chatraw, *Saving God's Green Earth: Rediscovering the Church's Responsibility to Environmental Stewardship* (Norcross, GA: Ampelon, 2006), 58, 140.

8. Brown, *Our Father's World*, 146.

9. "On the Care of Creation: An Evangelical Declaration on the Care of Creation" (1994), 2, http://www.earthcareonline.org/evangelical_declaration.pdf.

10. Au Sable Institute, excerpts from "A Christian Land Ethic Background" and "Plea for Christian Stewardship," prepared as a joint statement by the presenters of papers at Au Sable Forum 1987, http://www.webofcreation.org/DenominationalStatements/ausable.htm.

To Non-Christian Readers

1. Dan Story, *Where Wild Things Live: Wildlife Watching Techniques and Adventures* (Happy Camp, CA: Naturegraph, 2009).

2. Romans 1:20 (NLT).

3. Acts 17:24–27.

4. Psalm 19:1–4; Acts 14:16–17; 17:24–28; Romans 1:19–20.

5. Other writers who have explored this theme include C. S. Lewis, *The Weight of Glory and Other Addresses* (New York: HarperSanFrancisco, 2001); Alister McGrath, *Glimpsing the Face of God: The Searching for Meaning in the Universe* (Grand Rapids: Eerdmans, 2002) and *A Brief History of Heaven* (Oxford: Blackwell, 2003); Arthur O. Roberts, *Exploring Heaven: What Great Christian Thinkers Tell Us About Our Afterlife with God* (New York: HarperSanFrancisco, 2003).

6. Romans 8:19–22.

7. Isaiah 65:17–25 (see also 11:6–9); Revelation 21:1, 22:3–5.

8. Colossians 1:16–17; Hebrews 1:3.

9. Isaiah 51:3; Ezekiel 36:35.

DAN STORY (BA, San Diego Bible College; MA, Simon Greenleaf University) is the author of six books, including *Christianity on the Offense*, *Engaging the Closed Minded*, and *Defending Your Faith*. He has also written more than thirty nature/ecology-related articles and fifteen apologetic booklets. The former director and president of the non-profit Defending the Faith Ministries, Story has taught Sunday school classes, Bible studies, and college apologetics classes. Dan offers a variety of creation care and apologetic workshops and has been a guest on more than fifty radio programs nationwide and on TV.

Dan can be contacted at
www.danstory.net